FRAMINGHAM STATE COLLEGE

3 3014 00330 3643

D0024722

"Arkoun's Islam is tolerant, liberal and modern ... [His] vision embodies profound possibilities."

—NEW YORK TIMES BOOK REVIEW

RETHINKING ISLAM

Common Questions, Uncommon Answers

MOHAMMED ARKOUN

translated and edited by
Robert D. Lee

Westview Press

Rethinking Islam

RETHINKING ISLAM

ISLAM

*Common Questions,
Uncommon Answers*

MOHAMMED ARKOUN

translated and edited by
Robert D. Lee

WESTVIEW PRESS

Boulder • San Francisco • Oxford

Framingham State College
Framingham, Massachusetts

All rights reserved. No part of this publication may be reproduced or transmitted in any form or by any means, electronic or mechanical, including photocopy, recording, or any information storage and retrieval system, without permission in writing from the publisher.

English edition copyright © 1994 by Westview Press, Inc.

English edition published in 1994 in the United States of America by Westview Press, Inc., 5500 Central Avenue, Boulder, Colorado 80301-2877, and in the United Kingdom by Westview Press, 36 Lonsdale Road, Summertown, Oxford OX2 7EW

First published in 1989 in France by Jacques Grancher, Editeur, 98, rue de Vaugirard, 75006 Paris

Library of Congress Cataloging-in-Publication Data
Arkoun, Mohammed.
   [Ouvertures sur l'Islam. English]
   Rethinking Islam : common questions, uncommon answers /
Mohammed Arkoun ; translated and edited by Robert D. Lee
     p.   cm.
   Includes bibliographical references.
   ISBN 0-8133-8474-5 — ISBN 0-8133-2294-4 (pbk.)
   1. Islam—20th century.   I. Title.
BP163.A69613   1994
297—dc20   94-2485
                                                             CIP

Printed and bound in the United States of America

The paper used in this publication meets the requirements of the American National Standard for Permanence of Paper for Printed Library Materials Z39.48-1984.

10   9   8   7   6   5   4

BP
163
A69613
1994

Contents

v

Foreword

*C*hange has often swept in from the marches to overtake the center of the Islamic world. Islam first took root in Arabia on the periphery of two civilizations, the Roman, which dominated the Mediterranean area, and the Sassanian, which controlled lands to the east from its capital in Iraq. Arabs and Arabic prevailed in the new Islamic state, yet the development of Islamic civilization depended upon the contributions of non-Arabs and non-Muslims from the North and especially the East. Repeated waves of invaders drove across the Oxus River from central Asia to shake, destroy, and renew Islamic culture. The Ottoman state arose in the thirteenth century on the frontiers separating Islam from the Christian world, defended by the Byzantine Empire. And the most marginal of Islamic states, Spain, produced some of the most distinguished thinking and artistic activity of its age.

In the medieval era Muslims ruled the core of the Western world, the Mediterranean basin. Medieval Islamic cultures had absorbed innovation into the tradition, which came to include important elements of Greek medicine and philosophy, Persian literature, and Eastern mysticism. The onslaught of Western Crusaders, far from shaking the confidence of Muslims, merely reaffirmed their convictions of superiority and centrality. Centuries later, at the turn of the nineteenth century, Ottoman statesmen still believed that their society could exploit the strengths of the European world, such as industrial production of military weapons and experimental science, without compromising the integrity of their political, social, and cultural systems. To them, Europe remained marginal.

Then the periphery became the center, and the Islamic world found itself marginalized by European imperialism and universalism. Imperialism brought British and French troops, administrators, and merchants to the Middle East and imposed varying degrees of political, economic, and social subordination on the area. That process reached an apogee at Versailles after World War I, when the victors took it upon themselves to dismantle the defeated Ottoman Empire and establish a system of mandates for the governance of the Middle East. No Middle Easterner participated in the decisions. Faisal ibn Husayn, who attempted to attend on behalf of "the Arab State" the allies had promised to create, found himself shunted from one train to another and then from waiting room to waiting room. He languished on the margins, as did the entire Muslim world.

European universalism, while perhaps less visible than imperialism, was even more destructive to the Muslim world. Many parts of that world began to recover from imperialism in the period between the two wars, and by the end of World War II, independence broke out everywhere. The heightened importance of Middle Eastern oil, coupled with fresh discoveries in the 1950s and 1960s, provided a measure of economic autonomy enabling a few predominantly Muslim countries to reinforce their newly acquired political independence, but cultural dependence on Europe scarcely diminished. Although European liberalism had fallen into disfavor for its associations with European imperialism, European science, technology, and ideologies—such as nationalism, developmentalism, and Marxism—carried the day. Muslim elites espousing European ideas shoved the Islamic tradition to the margins of an otherwise marginalized world.

Mohammed Arkoun grew up on the fringes of the Arab, Islamic, and European worlds. He was born into a humble Berber family in the hillside village of Taourirt-Mimoun in the Kabylia, the so-called tribal region of Algeria. His family lived in the lower strata of the hillside village, both physically and socially; Taourirt-Mimoun itself was situated on the margins of successive dominant cultures and political configurations in Algeria, a country far removed from the heartland of Arabism and Islam. A native Berber speaker, Arkoun learned French as a second language, then Arabic as a third. A product of French schools and the French university system, he went on to teach Islamic history and philosophy at the Sorbonne. Having extracted himself from the outer reaches of Algerian society, he positioned himself at the edge of French academic life, then broadened his range of activity to Europe, America, Africa, and Asia.

Arkoun eschewed close association with the world of Western Orientalism, a discipline often linked to the European will to demean and dominate the Islamic world, but he also sought to avoid the clutches of nationalistic regimes all too eager to impose political and religious orthodoxy and to place restrictions on thought. He pushed to the very frontiers of Western social science in an effort to free Islam not just from Western misperceptions and misconceptions but also from the grips of many of its most fervent advocates. In so doing, he put himself on the cutting edge of Islamic discourse, or beyond it.

In the world Arkoun proposes, there would be no margins and no center, no marginalized groups and no dominant ones, no inferior beliefs and no superior, truth-producing logic. He seeks a response to what may be the critical political question of our time: How can people be thoroughly themselves without isolating themselves, by virtue of this identity, from their neighbors and the rest of humanity? He poses it for Muslims, in particular: Can the various Muslim identities be reconciled with each other and with non-Muslim identities, or does the contemporary reassertion of cultural identities mean the world is necessarily divided between Shi'is and Sunnis, mystics and traditionalists, Muslims and Christians, Berbers and Arabs, North Africans and Europeans? The implications of Arkoun's responses reach far beyond the world of Islam.

Events in Yugoslavia and the former Soviet Union in the early 1990s remind us that problems of identity are not limited to the Middle East, Africa, and South Asia.

Indeed, is there any country where problems of multiple identities have been thoroughly and permanently resolved? Canada, the United States, and Great Britain would all have difficulty making such a claim. But the clash between cultural identities and political order, both national and international, has been sharpest in the Third World and in predominantly Muslim countries. The reasons lie embedded in the history of Islam and in the history of the West. Arkoun would have us understand those histories as a means toward reconciling the universal with the particular, the oneness of human experience with the diversity of beliefs and identities that constitute the modern world.

The history of the West has been marked by increasing devotion to secular, rational, universalist ideals ever since the Renaissance. Despite countercurrents of romanticism, nihilism, and postmodernism, the West continues to propose a single, rational way of organizing an economy (the market), a single way of organizing the polity (liberal-democratic), and a single way of doing science (empirical). The technological power derived from these secular, rational, and universalist ideals overwhelmed the predominantly Muslim countries in the nineteenth and twentieth centuries. Elites in those countries came to view the West as the center of civilization and their own cultures as marginal vestiges of another epoch. Western Orientalists contributed to these perceptions by idealizing Islam in its medieval form. They tended to portray its belief structure and the societies embracing it as utterly different from Western structures and societies and, by extension, as thoroughly incompatible with modernity. Although they contributed enormously to Western knowledge of the Islamic world, the Orientalists also helped to marginalize both Islam itself and the more "deviant" Islamic practices within Islam.

Mohammed Arkoun's response to the threat of Europe-centeredness for Islamic identity goes beyond those of other Muslim writers. By the late nineteenth century, reformers such as Muhammad 'Abdu in Egypt were already rethinking Islam in light of modernity and colonial domination. Arkoun refers to these and other reformers as apologists, however courageous and enlightened, because they sought to prove that Islam had anticipated modern science, capitalism and socialism, and liberal democracy. For Arkoun, such apologists misread history by reading it backwards; they sought to counter Europe-centeredness with Islam-centeredness, perpetuating the idea that there is a single Islam with a single, superior, exclusive capacity for generating truth. Their reference point was still what Arkoun calls "Islamic reason," which, he argues, owes much to the Greeks and is no more tolerant of cultural and ideological diversity than are Western theories of modernization.

Much of Arkoun's vast scholarly production has concerned the tyranny of reason, Western and Islamic, and its impact on the image Muslims hold of themselves. He is critical of both East and West for believing in a superior form of reason because that belief cannot itself be defended by reason. He twits liberal democrats for neglecting their debt to Christian culture, and he condemns those Muslims who by virtue of superior knowledge claim to distinguish the "true" Islam from the false, the "true Muslim" from one who simply calls himself or herself a Muslim.

The claim of the contemporary Islamist movement is that reason must be subordinate to faith. The contemporary resurgence of Islam—whether on the West Bank or in Iran or Algeria—follows not from the reformist premise of the compatibility of Islam with Western reason but from the initial rejection of reason in the name of faith and the subsequent embrace of reason as a tool for the confirmation, clarification, and administration of that faith. What Arkoun identifies as a hidden premise in much of Islamic thought, the obsessive employment of Islamic reason, becomes explicit in the program of the Islamists. Their appeal lies in an explicit rejection of Western-centeredness and its replacement with a new, more rigorous, less tolerant version of Islam-centeredness. They presume to know who is or is not a "true Muslim" (the late president of Egypt, Anwar al-Sadat, and the late shah of Iran do not qualify as Muslims in their view), claiming a monopoly on truth. Westerners and all those who would continue to espouse either Western ideas or diverse views of Islam are relegated to the margins. For some groups, no Muslim is a "true Muslim" who does not seek to fight against "false" Muslims. For Arkoun, such a tyranny of faith is no more acceptable than the tyranny of reason.

Arkoun attempts to navigate through these dangerous shoals, between a Western universalism that tends to marginalize the entire Islamic tradition and an Islamic resurgence that puts itself at odds not only with Western tradition but also with the Islamic tradition as most Muslims have understood it for the past fourteen centuries. The principal compass he uses is history, but he also draws heavily on the tools of anthropology, semiotics, sociology, and postmodern philosophy. He tries to show that Islam has meant many things to many people at different epochs and that no logic permits dismissal of any of these views—not the superstitious worship of saint figures in a rural Algerian village, nor the philosophical inquiries of an Avicenna, nor the mysticism of cult groups—as un-Islamic.

For Arkoun, the history of Islamic society is inextricably linked with that of the West: There is no dichotomy between Western reason and Islamic reason. The two have fed upon each other. Both must be admired and mistrusted. Both must be viewed in the context of a single history of the "peoples of the Book/book," as he writes it, which regenerates universality without destroying particularity. In history lies Arkoun's hope of a world without margins.

History is, however, a great destroyer, as Nietzsche observed. Historicism pursued to its limits suggests that no ideals and no human actions can survive the erosion of time. Arkoun emphasizes the historicity of Islam, but the appeal of a religion such as Islam lies largely in its claim to offer eternal, transhistorical truth that has God as its source. Most Muslims believe that the Qur'an is not a created work, for if it were, one could speak about a time when God created it. Rather, they believe that the Qur'an is coeternal with God and hence beyond the reach of historical destruction. If Muslims came to understand Islam as a part of human history, as Arkoun proposes, would not its claim to truthfulness be washed away in the river of historical events?

Strangely and implausibly—this is the great interest of his work—Arkoun does not think so. He writes as a student of the "human sciences"—studies of the human condition carried on by human beings—who believes in the possibility of getting at expressions of truth shaped by history and shaping history. Underneath his painstaking analysis of medieval Islamic philosophy or modern militant Islamic movements there lies a deep emotional commitment to a better world based on a more comprehensive understanding of Islam and its historical relationship to Judaism and Christianity. He believes in the capacity of the human sciences to treat symbols and images as well as texts as part of the truth about religion; he entreats Muslims and non-Muslims alike to join in the reexamination of the "societies of the Book/book"—the societies of the Jewish, Christian, and Islamic traditions. Although Arkoun denies there is anything one might call "the true Islam," he suggests that one could with sufficient patience establish all that Islam has been, all that has been thought about it, and all that has remained unthinkable or unthought. And in the totality of this understanding lies an important set of truths about Islam that can serve as a point of fixity and identity for Muslims and also as a bridge to other societies of the Book/book. It is the place of the human sciences to restitch (*remembrer* is the word he uses) the fragmented Islamic tradition and reweave it into the broader cloth of the world of which it has always been a part. Such is Arkoun's highly ambitious enterprise.

The enterprise depends upon open discussion of sensitive issues in both West and East. In the West it involves a reexamination of the Orientalist tradition of Islamic studies, which has tended to portray Islam as divorced from the Western tradition by regarding it primarily as a set of texts and practices extracted from the dynamic of history; by implication, genuine understanding of Islam lies beyond the capacity of those who are not schooled in Arabic and deeply immersed in Islamic culture. Many fervent proponents of the Islamic tradition take similar positions. Part of the problem in both East and West is thus methodological and epistemological.

Another obstacle to such a rethinking of Islam is political. Arkoun has repeatedly said that no genuinely independent, creative work on the Islamic tradition can currently be done in the Arab world. The close ties between nationalist, authoritarian governments bent on using Islam for their own purposes or preoccupied with fending off militant, Islamist movements for equally clear reasons makes genuine scholarship impossible. The capacity of social science to generate the liberating truth about Islam depends upon a political atmosphere conducive to academic freedom and scientific discovery. Rethinking Islam depends upon the freedom to think; it must be done under liberal auspices, and thus, for now at least, it must be done in the West.

Arkoun puts himself squarely in the liberal camp but not without proposing a redefinition of liberalism. He argues that the Muslim world has shied from liberalism in part because of misconceptions generated and perpetuated in the West about the relationship between secularism and liberalism. For him, countries such as Turkey attempted to implement a model of liberalism fashioned from a simplistic reading of the Enlightenment. Arkoun follows contemporary analysts in suggesting that liberalism depends upon a religious tradition and not, as Mustafa Kemal (Atatürk) seems to have thought, upon the radical separation of politics and religion; he embraces liberalism on the condition that liberalism itself be reinterpreted.

Yet Arkoun, a liberal, is also a radical. His critiques of Western scholarship and traditional Islamic learning are equally devastating. He minces no words in his critique of those who would exploit Islam for ideological purposes, either to legitimize political aspirations or to delegitimize the efforts of others. In his campaign against marginality, he seeks to forge new links between faith and reason, subject and object, Islam, Judaism, and Christianity, Shi'ism and Sunnism, Europe and North Africa, East and West, North and South. In standing forthrightly for the notion that peoples be themselves in all their particularity without cutting themselves off from the rest of humanity, he dissociates himself from the predominant forces of our time: nationalism, ethnic separatism, Islamism. He projects a vision of Islam that clashes directly with that espoused officially in most of the Muslim world.

Yet he appeals to armies of scholars, not to men and women of the sword; his is a call for a revolution of the mind as a prelude and accompaniment to any possible political transformation. Perhaps that is one reason why his exposition of Islam has drawn less attention than that of Sayyid Qutb, mentor of the militant Islamist movement in Egypt, or of the Ayatollah Khomeini, theorist and leader of the Iranian revolution.

There are other reasons why Arkoun is less well known than he deserves to be. First, as a man working on the margins of Western academe and the margins of Islam, much of his early work appeared in journals of limited circulation. With one exception, his early books were compilations of journal articles. Second, his self-conscious methodology necessitated heavy use of social-scientific terminology, and his painstaking research on the Islamic tradition led him into a depth of detail quite beyond the reach of the general public. One needs a working knowledge of contemporary literature in the human sciences and considerable familiarity with Islamic history—not to mention good French—to appreciate much of what Arkoun has written.

This book, originally published in 1989 in French as *Ouvertures sur l'Islam,* constitutes his most concerted effort to reach a wider audience. It is based on his answers to twenty deceptively simple questions (e.g., "What do the words 'Muslim' and 'Islam' mean?" or "What did Muhammad want?") about Islam. In the second French edition of the book, published in 1992, Arkoun appended five articles. This translation is based on the second edition, but the additional materials have been edited into four additional chapters in the format of the original book. There are thus twenty-four questions and twenty-four straightforward but sophisticated responses. The answers provide basic information about the nature of Islam, but they also convey Arkoun's approach to the subject. The question-answer format introduces Islam to a general reader and, at the same time, introduces Arkoun's own notions of how Islam must be rethought if Muslims are to come to terms with themselves and with the rest of the world. The issue of identity—particularity and universality, marginality and centrality—lurks beneath all the questions and all the answers.

From the margins of the Islamic world and of Western academic discourse, Arkoun has become an increasingly central figure in the contemporary debate about

Islam. He has taught and lectured in many countries and on several continents. He is scholar and crusader, scientist and activist, believer and critic, historicist and idealist, liberal and radical, citizen of the Islamic world and citizen of Europe. His ideas merit the greater public and scholarly attention they have been receiving. The winds of change may again be blowing in from the marches.

Robert D. Lee
Colorado College

Acknowledgments

I would like to express my profound thanks to my colleague and friend Robert Lee, who, without having met me, wrote a piece about my work called "Arkoun and Authenticity."[1] He explained that his interest in my writings stemmed less from a desire to learn about Islam than from a desire to pursue an objective I associate with the sciences of human beings and society: to look at Islam in the context of a worldwide investigation of the mechanisms of production, reproduction, and control of meaning that are at work at different levels of human existence. Indeed, my ultimate goal, recommended to me by the claims of Islam, and for that matter by those of other religions, is to furnish and control the definitions and resources necessary to the comprehension of meaning.

Later, I met Robert Lee and we exchanged views in a way that proved fruitful for both of us and for our respective students. From our contact emerged the project of translating *Ouvertures sur l'Islam*. In addition to his familiarity with the literature of the social and political sciences, Robert Lee's command of French enabled him to produce a translation that respects both the stylistic demands of English and the conceptual content of my technical vocabulary. We decided not to use a literal translation of the French title, which would necessarily have been less rich in connotation than the original. *Rethinking Islam* is a translation of a title I used in 1986 for a keynote lecture at the Center for Arab Studies, Georgetown University: "Penser l'Islam aujourd'hui." The word "rethinking" may fall short of the critical force and programmatic approach suggested by the French, but it conveys the central thrust of my endeavor.

Mohammed Arkoun
Paris

Notes

1. *Peuples méditerranéens* 50 (January-March 1990), pp. 75–106.

Introduction

*T*his book was conceived, written, and published for a broad audience. Starting from topics of current interest, uncertainty, and prejudice in France and in Europe more generally, two French intellectuals formulated twenty questions for me concerning Islam and Muslims. The ongoing debate about the immigration of Turks into Germany, of Indians, Pakistanis, and Africans into Great Britain, and of North Africans, Lebanese, Syrians, and Africans into France, Belgium, and Holland has tended to transform cultural and scientific curiosity in these countries into a delineation of political positions, driven by rising emotions and tensions fraught with racist overtones. Confronting that situation, I sought with my responses to defuse the issue and to open intellectual, historical, anthropological, theological, and philosophical perspectives on Islamic studies, which have so often been confined in the West (Europe and North America) to static descriptions of beliefs, life-styles, images, institutions, and practices unique to "Islam" and "Muslims."

Specialists have done erudite, normative work on the encounter between the Islamic universe of thought and action and Christian Europe, modern and secular, but the general public knows little or nothing of that work. An imbalance has thus developed between the legitimate, concrete questions raised by a Western audience overwhelmed by the journalistic coverage of Muslim countries and the answers provided by classic Islamology, founded on the philological, historicist reading of old texts, or by political science, which is locked into short-term (ten- to twenty-year) analyses of events, actors, and stakes.

I have sought to liberate critical discourse on Islam and so-called Muslim societies[1] from all these limitations and contradictions by systematically choosing a *dynamic* vision rather than a *static* presentation, a bundle of methods taught by the social sciences rather than one method privileged over all others, and a comparative approach rather than the ethnographic view taken by those who tend to enclose and marginalize Islam in "specificity," particularism, and singularities. Islamic culture, in fact, is not reducible to the stereotypes articulated by the Christian religion and European cultures ever since the thirteenth century. Muslim apologists together with Islamic militants have transformed what is, in essence, an ideological specificity constructed by the Western scientific study of Islam into historical and doctrinal "authenticity" that only Islam has, in their view, managed to bequeath and preserve through the centuries and across the diverse sociocultural settings where it spread.

Thus I have geared my responses to do battle on two fronts: against the mythologization and ideologization of Islam proclaimed by militants of all sorts, by ulema who have become part of the state-nation-party establishment, and by contemporary Muslim apologists, and against what is often a static and fragmented portrayal of Islam that the great Western experts in Islamology continue to elaborate under the pretext that they are only faithfully transcribing the discourse, both ancient and contemporary, that Muslims have generated about their own religion and about their place in the great scheme of history.[2]

The two-front battle leads me into complexities, entanglements, fleeting allusions, and a technical terminology that both underscores the need for a "simple" book for a broad audience and reinforces my initial determination to write such a book. Many who have found value in the French, Arabic, and Dutch editions of this book are general readers who express regret at their inability to penetrate the debates and technical issues to be found in works more oriented toward the needs of specialists.

The project of constructing a historical and epistemological critique of the principles, postulates, definitions, conceptual tools, and discursive procedures of logical reasoning used in the Islamic context is a demanding first step in this two-front battle. The complexity of this task reflects an inextricable set of circumstances created by the build-up over centuries of the *unthought* in the exercise of Islamic thought.[3] It is not possible to break ground for new research on the prophetic discourse to be found in the major corpora of the three monotheistic religions without starting with the liberation of thought from all theories, dogmas, and imageries bestowed by the self-founding and self-proclaiming theologies of each community against its rivals. Then and only then can one tackle Islam itself in an inquiry of an anthropological character on the emergence, construction, expansion, and reproduction of beliefs in societies, whether religious with mythical points of reference or secular with rationalistic, historical requirements. This problematic brings together the short and long run, the comparative approach, the give-and-take between "global and local" as prescribed in the essays of Clifford Geertz, the historical and semiotic analysis of religious discourse *prior* to its theological exploitation for self-justifying purposes, and the opportunity to shift all our "knowledge" of Islam from the epistemological level that Michel Foucault calls the "historico-transcendental theme" to the level of postmodern reason, which has become critical of Enlightenment reasoning itself.

The great majority of Orientalists who specialize in the study of Islam remain indifferent to upheavals linked to the "postmodern condition."[4] Postmodernity generates models of historical action by which human beings change human beings more radically and more rapidly than in the theologizing or even the modernizing (secularizing) phase of history.

I believe Islam will not escape the upheavals of postmodernism. All the exegetical, theological, juridical, and semiotic constructs characteristic of classical Islam, now revived as fragments taken out of context or poorly situated in context as parts of what is called "contemporary Islam," will be affected.[5] The dynamic of postmodern history acts in helter-skelter, *unconsidered* fashion in the so-called Muslim societies of today; research, however, has not correctly integrated this dynamic into all levels and all domains of analysis.

How will the vast English-speaking public, Muslim and non-Muslim, respond to my positions, propositions, and perspectives on Islam in its period of emergence (610–661), classical elaboration (661–1258), repetition and scholastic fragmentation (1258–1800), and reactivation and political militancy in the nineteenth and twentieth centuries? All depends on the degree to which readers are sensitive to the concerns and practices of postmodern thought. Surely those who hold fast to postulates, hierarchies, and cleavages together with notions of truth, progress, and civilization bequeathed by the Enlightenment will react negatively to the glimpse of a new interpretation of the *Qur'anic fact* and the *Islamic fact* fashioned in the light of a cultural, social, and religious anthropology that has extended and reinterpreted the findings of historians, sociologists, and linguists. Arab readers have reacted positively to these ideas wherever their cultural circumstances have permitted them to step beyond what I call the "dogmatic closure" of Islamic thought—a closure prolonged and aggravated by the no less alienating closure characteristic of Arab, Turkish, and Iranian nationalisms, all imported and badly transplanted. That is to say that, alongside the "Muslim rage" described by Bernard Lewis[6] and the fundamentalist tendencies so obligingly observed, reported, and echoed in the Western media, there exists a liberal, critical Islam open to change, an Islam still little known and rarely taken into consideration.

As conceived and written, this book may present another difficulty that deserves clarification. The book does not fit easily into any category; it is neither vulgarizing literature aimed at a large audience nor erudite research of the sort published in scientific monographs. For this reason, Orientalists engaged in erudition may not deign to peruse a book that does not bring them new information, and even an enlightened public may find it difficult to fill in the blanks left by allusive references to events and ideas I take to be generally known. This dilemma afflicts any essay that aims to problematize a domain of knowledge, to think through and reflect upon historical circumstances, to deconstruct cognitive systems and ethico-juridical codes, and to historicize beliefs and nonbeliefs rather than to increase the mass of available data, rework interpretations, or extend the exploration of a single domain of reality.

These two types of mental activity and the resulting types of knowledge are no doubt both necessary and theoretically complementary. In practice, however, they continue to be treated as separate endeavors and are often seen as opposed to one other; "serious" research often rejects as methodological and epistemological claptrap the reflective activity required to get at the key concepts of a culture and each historical moment of its evolution. In any case, it is not a lack of information but an absence of reflection about the principles and founding values of the Islamic tradition that has permitted contemporary Islam to veer off into mythological and ideological detours.

The constraints that weigh on an essay of this sort in its efforts to implement a variety of analytical strategies lie not only in the field of Islamic tradition and thought but also in Western sources. Ever since the eighteenth century, Western thought has repeatedly challenged "Islam"—that is, the societies heavily influenced by Islam—to undergo conversion to modernity or to continue its regression toward a mythologized, disembodied, obsessive past. That means that the West has not accepted the challenge—or even the objection—that arises from within its own culture; even in the midst of a generalized crisis such as that opened by the end of Marxist eschatology, Western reason has maintained its pressure on the rest of the world and its refusal to entertain forms of thought coming from the outside. Thus, critical voices expressing solidarity with the history of Muslim peoples must constantly submit to demands that their arguments be more "objective," more "neutral," less "polemical," less engaged in recurrent forms of protest against the West. Such critics are repeatedly called upon to convert once and for all to the "values" of the West. In this fashion the history of the hegemonic world rolls on, perpetuating a sovereignty over human beings that was once attributed to God, while secondary actors exhaust themselves in imitating, adapting, reproducing, and confirming the productivity and insuperability of that world.

Europeans speak of the weaknesses of Enlightenment reasoning. They emphasize the crisis of political thought, the disappearance of all ethical discourse, the weakening of the philosophical quest for meaning, the deterioration of the providential welfare state, the increasing fragmentation and abstraction of literary and artistic production. Such criticism constitutes a part of the constant work of introspection by which Europe has built its greatness and extended its influence. But when Islamic thought points out the dangers of uncritical allegiance to these same forces of disintegration and alienation, Europeans tend to reaffirm the untouchability and universality of their model.

If we put the United States into this analysis of the cruel game of hegemonies and residual forces seeking to emerge or reemerge in history, everything gets more complicated and takes on a *tragic* intensity in the Greek sense: Inexorable powers, blind and indifferent to the question of meaning, make irreversible decisions about the destinies of whole peoples for indeterminate amounts of time. Despite the solemn commitments taken by Europe and the United States after the barbarisms of the Nazis and Stalin, who is doing anything to stop or even attenuate this recurrent tragedy afflicting every part of the globe?

Notes

1. When Arkoun refers to "so-called" Muslim societies, he means to suggest that this terminology, however widespread, is inaccurate because it brands whole societies with a label that may be helpful in explaining the behavior of only some members of those societies some of the time. Generalizations about "Muslim societies" may not be any more helpful than global statements about "Christian societies," but the former certainly outnumber the latter in Western writing.—TRANS.

2. I refrain from naming colleagues, who are after all entitled to personal opinions. I do not seek in any way to minimize or ignore the positive, innovative contributions of their work.

3. Arkoun means aspects of the Islamic tradition that have not been analyzed or "thought" but merely accepted.—TRANS.

4. Jean-François Lyotard, *The Postmodern Condition: A Report on Knowledge,* translated by Geoff Bennington and Brian Massumi (Minneapolis: University of Minnesota, 1984).

5. The operations by which social actors decontextualize ideas, beliefs, and doctrines advanced by their culture out of context and then recontextualize them deserves long analysis for the case of Islam. The Qur'an, for example, has been ripped from its historical, linguistic, literary, and psychological contexts and then continually recontextualized in various cultures and according to the ideological needs of various actors. This comment, though trivial for the historian, the linguist, and the anthropologist, is rejected by the theologian and understood poorly if at all by the ordinary believer. But have we not also seen intellectuals, who are in theory converted to the notion of critiquing all mechanisms for the production of meaning, commit multiple anachronisms?

6. See Bernard Lewis, "The Roots of Muslim Rage," *The Atlantic Monthly,* September 1990.

❧ 1 ❧

Imagining Islam

Can one speak of a scientific understanding of Islam in the West or must one rather talk about the Western way of imagining Islam?

*I*n a small book designed for a broad Western audience, it is useful and even necessary to start with this question. We can, in fact, wonder whether the Western understanding of Islam is valid and objective. Ever since the 1950s, when national liberation movements emerged, there have been continual debates on this issue, many of them sharp and passionate. If I evoke the war for Algerian independence (1954–1962), for example, every French person who was alive then remembers the accompanying polemics and deadly confrontations about the Arab world and Arab culture generally seen in the context of Nasserism, the emergence of the Third World at the Bandung Conference of 1955, and the Zionist struggle for the establishment of the state of Israel. The links of these polemics to religious and political quarrels dating from the Middle Ages augmented their propensity to provoke violence.

The Algerian war ended, but the polemics continued as a result of other events, such as the revolution in Iran. The Ayatollah Khomeini's rise to power produced a fresh outpouring of emotions around the world, most notably in the United States, which exerts an influence in the Middle East that is widely recognized. The Iranian revolution touched vital Western interests in the Middle East, and the reactions that event provoked and continues to provoke have revived and enriched the Western way of "imagining" Islam. The Gulf War constituted yet another climax in the confrontation between two collective imaginaries: the Arab-Islamic and the Western.

The notion of "imagining" evoked in the question is new; the nonspecialist is not likely to grasp it, for even the experts have not succeeded in mastering the shape, function, and operation of this faculty we call imagination. To be brief, I will say that the "imaginary" of an individual, a social group, or a nation is the collection of images carried by that culture about itself or another culture—once a product of epics, poetry, and religious discourse, today a product primarily of the media and secondarily of the schools.[1] In this sense, of course, individuals and societies have their own imaginaries tied to their own common languages. There are thus French, English, and German ways of imagining Islam—imaginaries, as they have come to be called—just as there are Algerian, Egyptian, Iranian, and Indian imaginaries of the West. Since the 1950s the powerful, omnipresent media, drawn daily to report on the violent happenings of the moment—national liberation movements, protests, and revolts in the numerous and diverse countries inhabited by Muslims—have fed the Western imaginary of Islam.

The misperceptions inherent in this imaginary go beyond current events. Although the problems of Muslim societies have indeed become knottier and more numerous since the emergence of national states in the 1950s and 1960s, another serious confusion—one that has contributed directly to the shaping of the Western imaginary of Islam—has also emerged in this short time. That is, all the political, social, economic, and cultural shortcomings of Muslim societies are hitched together and to Islam with a capital "I." Islam then becomes the source and the prime mover of all contemporary history in a world that extends from the Philippines to Morocco and from Scandinavia, if we take account of Muslim minorities in Europe, to South Africa.

It is true that the sort of Islamic discourse common to fundamentalist movements, especially those engaged in the most decisive political battles, proposes the powerful image of a single, eternal Islam, the ideal model for historic action to liberate the world from the Western, imperialist, materialist model. The media in the West seize upon this monolithic, fundamentalist view of Islam that dominates the contemporary Muslim imaginary and transpose it into a discourse suitable to the social imaginary of Western countries without any intermediate critique from the social sciences. The field of perception is open to the confrontation of two imaginaries overheated by accumulated confusions about each other.

This everyday labor of stimulating and amplifying the two imaginaries is complicated by a much older and more serious issue, one that reaches to the most sacred origins of the three monotheistic religions. Ever since the emergence of Islam between 610 and 632, there has been continuous rivalry among three religious communities—Jewish, Christian, and Muslim—all striving to establish a monopoly on the management of symbolic capital linked to what the three traditions call "revelation." The issue is enormous and primordial, yet it has nonetheless been buried by secularized, ideological discourse: the ideologies of nation building, scientific progress, and universal humanism in nineteenth- and twentieth-century Europe. Then, beginning with the Nazi catastrophe and the wars of colonial liberation, the question of revelation was buried under the no less deceptive rhetoric of decolonization, of development and underdevelopment (in the 1960s), and of nation building in Third World countries that had just recovered their political sovereignty.

To this day, *no one* has studied revelation in its Hebrew, Aramaic, and Arab manifestations and as a function of the historical and anthropological conditions for the emergence of these three traditions. That constitutes a failure of the comparative history of religions, of social science, and of the human sciences, which have left the task of "managing the goods of salvation" to the theologians of each community. That is to say that they have perpetuated theological discourse in its function of legitimating the drive for power of each community. This fact condemns discourse to the confines of a cultural system that excludes all those others who have the sacrilegious pretension to draw upon the same symbolic capital.

It may seem excessive to claim that revelation has not been studied *anywhere* in its three historical manifestations, while an immense literature on the subject clutters the shelves of our libraries. I want to emphasize, however, the following evidence: In constructing a Judeo-Christian vision of the story of salvation, Christianity, on both the Catholic and the Protestant sides, annexed the Old Testament to the New in such a way that Jews protested the dissolving of their Talmudic and prophetic tradition; as for Muslims, they remained excluded from this theological structure by the fact that Islam follows Christianity chronologically and because the structure portrays Jesus Christ as the final expression of the Word of God. Already in Medina between 622 and 633 A.D., Jews and Christians refused to recognize Muhammad as a prophet in the same spiritual line as Moses and Jesus in salvation history.[2]

To this historical evidence must be added the abdication of the social and human sciences, loath to take on all the disputes bequeathed by theological structures as problems of religious and anthropological history. I can testify that these problems have not yet been approached in a comparative perspective combining history and cultural-religious anthropology. Islam is always considered apart from other religions and from European culture and thought. It is often excluded from departments of religion and taught instead as a part of Oriental studies.

Another aggravating factor in the old quarrel between Islam and the West is that Islam, as a force in the historical rise of societies, took control of the Mediterranean area from the seventh to the twelfth centuries and again, with the direction of the Ottoman Turks, from the sixteenth to the eighteenth centuries. The cultures of the Mediterranean region share a single historical destiny that the scientific study of history, independent of the ideologies that divide the northern and southern or the eastern and western coasts of the Mediterranean, is far from confronting. The Mediterranean region I refer to is more cultural than geographic and strategic; it encompasses all those cultures that have been influenced historically by Iranian religions and the great ancient cultures of the Near East, including the Mesopotamian, the Chaldean, the Syriac, the Aramaic, the Hebraic, and the Arabic—all before the intervention of Greece, Rome, Byzantium, and "Islam."

I should note in passing the influence of the vocabulary used to evoke the plurality of cultures in the Near East. In speaking of the Aramaic, the Syriac, and the Byzantine, I am including Christianity. In speaking of the Hebraic, I am referring to the Jewish religion. But Islam, linked of course to Arabic, designates both the religion begun by Muhammad and the vast empire quickly built by the new power center in Damascus, which shifted to Baghdad and Cordoba. For this reason I have put quotation marks around the word "Islam."

The confusion between Islam as religion and Islam as historical framework for the elaboration of a culture and a civilization has been perpetuated and has grown ever more complex to this day. Nonetheless, Islamic societies must be examined in and for themselves, as French, German, Belgian, U.S., or Polish societies are. It is certainly legitimate for research to identify common factors that generate a single Islamic discourse in very different societies, but then it must also come back to the history of each of these societies and to its own culture. It is important to identify the ideological obstacles that retard the study of the Mediterranean area as a whole and obscure its pertinence to a modern revival of the history of religions, philosophy, and cultures.

The lesson provided by Fernand Braudel in his great book, *The Mediterranean and the Mediterranean World in the Age of Phillip II,*[3] has not carried so far as to modify history curricula in high schools and universities. The southern and eastern coasts of the Mediterranean continue to be the domain of specialists in Arabic and Turkish studies—that is to say, of that nebulous "science" we call Orientalism. What is taught about the Arab or Muslim Mediterranean is highly conditioned by the European perspective on the Mediterranean world.

The European perspective has itself been relegated to the background ever since the U.S. Seventh Fleet established strategic control of the whole of the Mediterranean area extending to Iran. Meanwhile, Europe has dedicated all its resources and energies to the construction of a community in which Germany, a country utterly foreign to Mediterranean culture, occupies a central position. Will the presence in the European Community of Greece, Spain, and Portugal eventually reestablish a long-lasting and effective interest in the Mediterranean dimension of the Community by including Arab and Islamic contributions in the powerful, dynamic history of European construction? These are crucial political and cultural issues for the coming decade. It is clear that definitive peace between Israel and the Palestinians would generate hope of almost apocalyptic dimensions for all peoples in the Mediterranean sphere of influence.

I aim here only to reestablish proper historical perspective on the political, economic, and strategic stakes of the unending wars around the Mediterranean. More fundamentally, the task of historians of religions, cultures, and philosophy is to show how ethnocultural groups of varying size and dynamism have dipped into the common stock of signs and symbols to produce systems of belief and nonbelief that, all the while assigning ultimate meaning to human existence, have served to legitimate power drives, hegemonic empires, and deadly wars. All "believers," whether they adhere to revealed religions or contemporary secular regions, would thus be *equally* constrained to envisage the question of meaning not from the angle of unchanging transcendence—that is, of an ontology sheltered from all historicity—but in the light of historical forces that transmute the most sacred values, those regarded as most divine by virtue of their symbolic capital and as inseparable from necessarily mythical accounts of the founding, and from which each ethnocultural group extracts and recognizes what it calls identity or personality.

It is in this new field of intelligibility, beyond the dogmatic definitions that continue to safeguard the mobilizing, ideological force of revealed religions, that the phenomenon of revelation must be reexamined. Only when this perspective holds sway will multidisciplinary and crossdisciplinary analysis of a phenomenon with many faces and functions penetrate to the *radical imaginary*[4] common to the societies of the *Book/books.*

First, though, we need to revise history textbooks in France, Germany, Belgium, the United States, and elsewhere. We must acknowledge the intellectual and cultural poverty of the brief chapters devoted to Islam in high school courses. As for the universities, rare are those even now with history departments willing to tolerate the intrusion of a historian of Islam.[5] The teaching of the history of "Islamic cultures"[6] is all too often left to the department of so-called Oriental languages, where one exists. This observation, which holds for most universities in the West, demonstrates the extent to which an ideological vision of the history of the Mediterranean area has been translated administratively and institutionally into the universities themselves. And the field is open for essayists and journalists to construct imagery of Islam and Muslims based on current events and locked into a short-term perspective dominated by Nasserism, Khomeinism, Israel, and the Palestinians.

To be fair in this description of mutual perceptions of "Islam" (I repeat: This global designation of multiple and different realities is very dangerous; hence I use quotation marks) and of "the West" (another, no less dangerous global designation[7]), I must speak briefly of the situation from the Muslim side. First I must distinguish the perceptual framework of classical Islam from that of contemporary Islam. For classical Islam, the inhabited world was theologically and juridically divided between the home of Islam (*dār al-islām*), where the Divine Law applied, and the land of war (*dār al-ḥarb*), where "infidels" always threatened to substitute "pagan" laws for the True Law, as they did in Mecca and Medina in the time of the Prophet. (A similar division existed for Christianity before Vatican II in 1965.) The Divine Law, revealed in the Qur'an,[8] was rendered explicit and applied by the Prophet and the so-called "orthodox caliphs" in Medina from 622 to 661, and for the Shi'a by the line of designated Imams. From this division of the world into two parts came a special status for "protected peoples" (*dhimmī*), Jews and Christians recognized as peoples of the Book (*ahl al-kitāb*) but as theologically beyond the "community promised salvation" (*al firqa al-nājiya*). Today's Jews and Christians are wrong to use this status as a theme of polemics against today's Muslims; they should rather deal with this problem as historians would, avoiding the anachronism of projecting the philosophy of human rights and religious liberty—conquered late in the West (French Revolution) on a theoretical level and still incompletely and randomly applied on a practical level—onto a theological mentality *common* to the three revealed religions.

The theological vision similarly divides time into *before* and *after* the founding moment of the new salvation history. Jews, Christians, and Muslims thus have their respective eras, and all face this question about the theological position of human beings who lived before the "final" revelation was manifest.

Understanding that space and time are for all human beings the coordinates of every perception of an object of knowledge, one can measure the impact of theological systems on all modes of intelligibility in the societies of the Book, where the revealed, Holy Book has engendered all other books containing the knowledge constitutive of each cultural "tradition." Scholars have not yet abandoned these frameworks of perception, and my observation about textbooks and departments of history shows how the conditions for intelligibility in a desacralized, secularized time and space carry forward in ideological form the prevailing distinctions established by religions.

Inside theological space and time, Muslim geographers of the classical epoch wrote and taught "profane" perceptions of peoples and cultures outside the Muslim domain.[9] What is interesting about this vast geographical literature is its demonstration that the miraculous—hence, the imaginary—intervenes in the perception and the definition of the *other*. To describe the construction of an image of the other as a psychocultural process tied to typical histories and frameworks of intelligibility is an intriguing *new* practice of scientific history.

What can be said now about the perception of the "West" by contemporary "Islam"?

One of the first breaks with classical frameworks goes back to an Egyptian traveler in France in the nineteenth century, Rifa'a al-Tahtawi, who left a moving account of his "discoveries" in a France freshly emerged from revolutionary battles and Napoleonic wars. His view is positive, admiring, and uneasy. The contrast between a free, dynamic society open to change and a Muslim society that was repetitive, conformist, and conservative touched off a desire for progress, reform, and revision. Despite brutal colonial conquests, notably in Algeria, Western civilization stunned him, provoking admiration and envy. It elicited an irrepressible desire for change and movement in Muslim society. Political, literary, artistic, and university figures opened themselves to the lessons of Enlightenment philosophy. They believed they could lead Muslim societies along the same historical course the West had followed toward a civilization perceived as superior, effective, and liberating.

In the years between 1920 and 1940, a secular nationalist movement supported by a reformist Islamic current began to oppose the liberals, who favored imitation of the Western cultural model. The reformist movement, tracing itself back to Jamal al-Din al-Afghani and Muhammad 'Abdu in the nineteenth century, continued and grew with the Muslim Brotherhood in Egypt and with the Association of Reformist Ulema in Algeria. The rivalry between the liberal and reformist-nationalist positions took a decisive turn with the end of World War II, the creation of the state of Israel, and the coming to power of the Free Officers and Nasserism in Egypt in July 1952. During the Algerian war, which began in November 1954, a nationalist, anticolonial, anti-imperialist, and anti-Zionist perspective gradually took the place of the liberal view held by small "Westernized" groups with their naïve, depoliticized conception of cultural transformation in Muslim societies.

To complete this picture, I would have to recount the stories of Nasserism's confrontations with the demands of the Muslim Brothers, of the confrontation between Atatürk's secularism and a Europe looking for political hegemony and economic domination, of Bourguibism in its struggle for Westernization in the framework of Tunisia's reacquired political sovereignty, of the populist revolution eager to take shortcuts to industrialize, Arabize, and Islamicize Algerian society in a single historic movement, and of Ba'athist socialism in Syria and Iraq, which aimed to build the Arab nation by combining bits and pieces of Enlightenment philosophy with a romantic version of Islam and a projection of Arab culture back onto the legacy (*turāth*) of the classical age, also called the Golden Age, of Arab-Islamic civilization.

All these movements enjoyed fleeting success owing to the availability of peoples still sensitive to Messianic promises and eschatological expectations. The leaders who benefited from this availability did not perceive the corrosive action and devastating effects of their *ideological* discourse, which substituted unrealizable political programs for the millenary, transhistorical hopes nourished by the *mythical* discourse of traditional religion.[10]

The emergence of Khomeini and the eruption of "Islamic" revolution in Iran in 1979 brought a new illustration of the distinction, not only for the case of Islam but also for other historical trajectories. When Khomeini used "Islamic" discourse to regenerate the ethos of Shi'ite consciousness and to eliminate the "Pharaonic" regime of the shah, he benefited from the disappointed hopes of Arab and Muslim peoples, who had been mobilized ever since the 1950s by socialist-inspired ideologies such as Ba'athism. The confusion between mythical religious discourse and mobilizing, desanctifying ideological discourse reached maximum mobilizational efficacy and destructive effect on the semantic ordering of the community. It produced a particularly dangerous inversion of values, because the most engagés of social actors understood this regeneration of Shi'ite consciousness as social promotion. What was presented as restoration of "Islamic" legitimacy for power, law, and ethical values proved to be only a tragic parody of the formal practices of "democracy" cut off from Islamic principles of authority and foundational philosophy for the rights of man.

With the dissipation of the mythical force of the Arab nation and the Arab Socialist revolution as models for the liberation of other peoples of the Third World, all of a sudden religious consciousness has been demythologized not by historicizing religious knowledge[11] but through ideological manipulation of popular belief and of the richest parts of the tradition. In a great historic drama, Muslim peoples were brutally confronted with material civilization and intellectual modernity. Neither the "Socialist revolution" (in its Nasserist and Algerian phase) nor the "Islamic revolution" (in its Iranian phase) reflected a powerful movement of philosophical and scientific criticism of the religious tradition, of political practice in the inherited culture, or of the problem of knowledge in general; there was nothing to compare in these regards with the eighteenth-century movement that prepared the way for the French Revolution. When in the 1950s and 1960s Nasser sent the Muslim Brothers to prison and even had them hung, he was not thereby encouraging a modernization of Islamic consciousness; likewise, Boumediene in Algeria after 1965 simultaneously fostered slogans of Socialist revolution and spectacular, official operations to traditionalize society with a "return" to ritual, fragmentary expressions of Islam. With the "Islamic revolution," the restoration of the law and ritual practice is more systematic, but the crucial problems inherited from what I call the exhaustive Islamic tradition[12] are further than ever removed from scientific and philosophical examination.

The *unthought* and the *unthinkable* in Islamic thought have been accumulating ever since ideologies of struggle for political liberation took over the whole of the social arena. Forced to forswear colonial domination, the West has since the 1960s launched a search for new expressions of modernity, while the Muslim world has, quite to the contrary, turned away from these opportunities and proposed instead an "Islamic" model, which is beyond all scientific investigation. This notion constitutes the triumph of a social imaginary that is termed "Islamic" but that in fact sacralizes an irreversible operation of political, economic, social, and cultural secularization. Analysts have barely noticed this new role of Islam used at the collective level as an instrument of disguising behaviors, institutions, and cultural and scientific activities inspired by the very Western model that has been ideologically rejected.

We must try, as we go along, to *rethink* the historical situation created by the evolution of Muslim societies during the past thirty years. We must linger over those problems rendered *unthinkable* by the ideology of struggle in the hope of opening a new historic phase in this process of evolution, a phase where critical thought—anchored in modernity but criticizing modernity itself and contributing to its enrichment through recourse to the Islamic example—should accompany, or even for once precede, political action, economic decisions, and great social movements.

Notes

1. For an extensive discussion of the "imaginary," see Cornelius Castoriadis, *The Imaginary Institution of Society,* translated by Kathleen Blamey (Cambridge: Polity, 1987). Castoriadis offers this initial effort at definition, p. 127: "Recall the common meaning of the term 'imaginary', which is sufficient for the moment: we speak of the 'imaginary' when we want to talk about something 'invented'—whether this refers to a 'sheer' invention ('a story entirely dreamed up'), or a slippage, a shift of meaning in which available symbols are invested with other significations than their 'normal' or canonical significations. ('What are you imagining now?' says the woman to the man who is chiding her for a smile she exchanged with someone else.) In both cases, it is assumed that the imaginary is separate from the real, whether it claims to take the latter's place (a lie) or makes no such claim (a novel)."

2. "Salvation history" is a translation of the term *Heilsgeschicte,* first used by J. C. von Hofman (1810–1877) "to refer to those events which the Bible narrates as manifesting God's deeds for the salvation of the world." That history would include creation, exodus, covenant, ancient Israel, the prophets, and the advent of the New Testament, among other events. Thomas P. McCreesh, "Salvation History," *The New Dictionary of Theology* (Wilmington: Michael Glazier, 1988). Other possible translations of the German term would be "history of salvation," "redemptive history," and "holy history." The term in French is *histoire du salut.*—TRANS.

3. Fernand Braudel, *The Mediterranean and the Mediterranean World in the Age of Phillip II* (London: Collins, 1972).

4. Castoriadis says: "To the extent that the imaginary ultimately stems from the originary faculty of positing or presenting oneself with things and relations that do not exist, in the form of representation (things and relations that are not or have never been given in perception), we shall speak of a final or radical imaginary as the common root of the actual imaginary and of the symbolic. This is finally the elementary and irreducible capacity of evoking images" (*The Imaginary Institution of Society,* p. 127).—TRANS.

5. When the great historian Claude Cahen retired in 1979, his chair in Oriental History at Paris I (Panthéon-Sorbonne) simply disappeared.

6. Cultures where Islam has been practiced and where Muslims have left their imprint are often called Islamic cultures. Arkoun uses quotation marks to remind us that much of what happens in such cultures is secular, un-Islamic, or even anti-Islamic in the eyes of many believers or simply explicable in terms of local customs quite unrelated to Islam.—TRANS.

7. I would distinguish the Christian West from the lay or secular West, but both terms are open to question as result of the planet-wide gestation of a single world of technology and communication.

8. Note that the Arabic word has often been transliterated in Western languages as "Koran" or "Coran." In the system of transliteration employed in this work, "qur'ān" is the most accurate rendering. That spelling will be used when Arkoun uses it in the lowercase. As the name of a literary work it will be written as "Qur'an."—TRANS.

9. I refer here to the rich new work of my friend and companion in intellectual combat, André Miquel, who has published four volumes on human geography in the Muslim world called *La géographie humaine du monde musulman jusqu'au milieu du XIᵉ siècle* (La Haye: Mouton, 1963–1988). To André Miquel's great credit, his work has caused an important sector of Arab cultural production to benefit from methods and problematics of history conceived and understood as an anthropology of a particular past and an archaeology of collective consciousness.

10. For more on this distinction, see my *Pour une critique de la raison islamique* (Paris: Maisonneuve et Larose, 1984), pp. 205–215. I intend to come back at greater length to this topic in a forthcoming book.

11. See Rudolf Bultmann, *History and Eschatology* (Edinburgh: Edinburgh University, 1975).

12. See "L'Islam actuel devant sa tradition," in *Aspects de la foi de l'Islam* (Brussels, 1985), translated as "Background Essay: Current Islam Faces Its Tradition," in *Architecture Education in the Islamic World* (The Aga Khan Award for Architecture, 1986).

✿ 2 ✿

Islam and Muslims

What do the words "Islam" and "Muslim" mean?

Usually the word *islām* is translated as "submission," "submission to God," or even "resignation." "Resignation" is quite inappropriate. Believers are not resigned before God. They experience outpourings of love toward God, a transformation pulling them toward acceptance of that which God proposes, because God, by revelation, raises human beings to his own level. This elevation elicits a human feeling of gratitude toward a Creator who has heaped creatures with good things. There is thus established a relationship of loving and grateful obedience between Creator and creature.

Etymologically, in Arabic the word *islām* means "to give something over to someone." Here it is a matter of "giving one's whole self over to God," of "entrusting all of oneself to God." Another meaning of the word *islām,* pointed up by historians of the language, fits well with the way it was originally used in the Qur'an: "to defy death" in giving over one's soul, that is to say one's life, to a noble cause. To give over one's soul, to give oneself in sacrifice, as, for example, in a battle on behalf of God, is to demonstrate in extreme fashion the sort of outpouring of love, the sort of transformation, that leads the believer to accept without reservation God's call and God's teachings. To move toward God is to move toward the absolute, toward transcendence; it is to feel promoted to a higher level of existence. All these connotations attach to the word *islām.*

There are several verses in the Qur'an where Abraham is introduced as a *muslim. Muslim* in the Qur'an refers to someone who acts in loving obedience to God, exemplified by Abraham's gesture in agreeing to God's request to sacrifice his son. When the Qur'an says that Abraham was neither a Jew nor a Christian but a *muslim,* it clearly does not refer to Islam as defined by the theologians and jurists in their interpretations of the Qur'an and the teachings of Muhammad. In that context, *Muslim* rather indicates an ideal religious attitude symbolized by Abraham's conduct in conformity with the Pact or Covenant (*mīthāq*) described in the Bible and the Qur'an. It is for this reason that Abraham is called the Father of Believers. He incarnates the founding religious attitude of monotheism *before* the establishment of rituals and legislation that would eventually define and particularize the three monotheistic religions. This initial religious attitude—the basis of the Covenant not in historical time and addressable space but in the infinite time-space of consciousness, an attitude

15

elicited by the absolute, beyond all influence of language, law, or tradition—in Arabic and in the Qur'an is called *islām*. In the Qur'an this word had already begun to acquire ritual, legislative, and semantic characteristics that the theologian-jurists later amplified and systematized into a corpus of belief and nonbelief that would become the Muslim religion, also called Islam.

This distinction between the *islām* of Abraham, reaffirmed in the religious experience of Muhammad, and the historical Islam of the theologian-jurists has a parallel in other terms used in the Qur'an: on the one hand, *umm al-kitāb* ("the mother of the book"), referring to the celestial Book, the archetype containing the inaccessible, mysterious totality of the Word of God; on the other, *al-kitāb* ("the book"), *al-qur'ān* ("the reciting"), *al-dhikr* ("the account"), and *al-furqān* ("the distinction between right and wrong")—all words used to designate the book as manifest in history, the Word as communicated to men and subsequently enmeshed in the terrestrial history of God's creatures. The Word transcribed by human hands onto parchment or paper is collected into a bound book, a *mushaf,* that one manipulates, transports, reads, and interprets in order to define Islam, the religion lived by Muslims, who are indistinguishably both believers and historical actors engaged in political, social, and ideological struggles. The same distinction can be made between Christ as word incarnate of God and the New Testament as accounts of the Word of God, collected in book form, by and for Christians, who are both believers *and* participants in history.

These distinctions could carry us far toward a modern theological revival, starting from the concept of revelation and moving in the context of a comparative theology that goes beyond polemics and beyond the exchange of artificial expressions of tolerance characteristic of so many meetings between Christians and Muslims since Vatican II in 1965. I will come back to this distinction between the Qur'anic fact and the Islamic fact, corresponding to the evangelical fact and the Christian fact, the biblical fact and the Jewish fact.[1] But the distinction between Islam and Muslim has another practical implication. Without paying much attention, many people use "Islamic world" to mean the same thing as "Muslim world," and, what is worse, books appear under the title "Islam" that treat history, culture, and societal institutions ranging from Indonesia to Morocco. Who would dare to describe the European societies as a group, even though they are predominantly inhabited by Christians, under the title "Christianity and Its Civilization," or "The Civilization of Classical Christianity"? (For these examples I have reworked the titles of two widely distributed books about Islam.)[2] It is true that even from its early Qur'anic phase the religious perspective mixed with profane concerns so that Islamic thought came to claim that the interweaving of the religious, the profane, and the political is characteristic of Islam. (In Arabic one refers to these three domains as *dīn, dunyā,* and *dawla.*) Faced with the separation of the religious and the temporal in Christianity, Islam still wants to base politics and society on religious teachings. But such an effort constitutes policy, not fact. To speak of societies as "Muslim" rather than as "Islamic" is to say quite simply that they are inhabited largely by Muslims. The use of the word "Islamic" to describe highly diverse societies must be avoided.

It is time we fostered a critical, scientific examination by each "Muslim" society of itself. Islam as a religion would thus be liberated from problems and responsibilities that are the exclusive province of social actors, not of God. To free societies from false gods would serve at the same time to extricate the divine from the phantasms to which human beings everywhere dedicate themselves with recurrent inventiveness.

Notes

1. See Mohammed Arkoun, *La pensée Arabe* (Paris: Presses Universitaires, 1975), chap. 1. Translated as *Arab Thought* by Jasmer Suigh (New Delhi: Chand, 1988). See also Arkoun, *Lectures du Coran* (Paris: Maisonneuve et Larose, 1982; 2nd ed., Tunis, 1991), introduction.

2. André Miquel, *L'Islam et sa civilisation* (Paris: Armand Colin, 1982); Dominique and Janine Sourdel, *La Civilisation de l'Islam classique,* 4th ed. (Paris: Arthaud, 1984).

⚜ 3 ⚜

Church and State

Does the separation of church and state, fundamental to secular ideology in the Western world, have its origin in the New Testament distinction: "Render to God that which is God's and to Caesar that which is Caesar's"?

*T*hat dictum is indeed cited very frequently on each occasion that Christians and Muslims try to compare the respective experiences of Islam and Christianity. But those who cite this saying of Christ must remember the historical conditions in which any religion, and even any theology in the broadest sense, emerges. The saying can indeed be understood only if we recall that Palestine in the time of Christ was under Roman authority. The political order was linked to the Roman Empire, and there was a Roman governor in Palestine who represented legal, legitimate political authority. (Legitimate in the eyes of Rome, of course!) As a result, the religious establishment could take no political initiative without referring to Rome. In this context, the only means for a man of religion to affirm any authority whatsoever was to remain entirely within spiritual and religious planes. And that is why, in effect, the words of Jesus laid claim to the spiritual prerogative that belonged to the prophets or to Jewish sacerdotal authority such as it was exercised in the synagogue among the Jews. By so doing, Jesus carried out two decisive operations. Although he did not directly attack Roman political power, he implicitly raised the question of its legitimacy, since that power was not founded on the spiritual authority of this God revealed in the person of Christ. As a result of his assertion about separation, tension arose between the Christian community and the rabbis on the one hand and the Roman authorities on the other.

Roman law constitutes a cultural creation so important that the whole history of the church in the West has been marked by it. The church claimed a right to supervise the exercise of political power on the basis of the spiritual authority bestowed on it by Christ. The tensions resulting from that claim led eventually to the English revolution and the execution of Charles I in 1649, to the French Revolution and the execution of Louis XVI in 1793, and to the legal separation of church and state. The French example is the most radical.

What was ultimately at stake in those developments was the distinction between power and authority. Authority arises from persuasion, from the conversion of consciousness to that which gives meaning to the existence of the person. There must be a free movement of the heart, as the Qur'an says, to obey a voice that elevates the person by the meaning it gives to his or her existence. This voice is that of God, of the Prophet, of the hero, of the leader, of the scholar, of the spiritual master, of the saint, or of the philosopher.

In each case there is optimal communication between two conscious beings, two subjects. There is a diminution of what Marcel Gauchet[1] calls the "debt of meaning." For the true meaning I assign to my existence, I am in debt to some authority who becomes a guide and whom I consent to obey; I internalize the commandments of the guide; I respect his *power* so long as it is exercised within the limits of *meaning* that he reveals to me as *authority*. This is exactly the relationship I analyzed with regard to the *islām* of Abraham. The revealed religions brought the notion of covenant to cover the *debt of meaning* through an exchange of authority and loving obedience in a context of completely reciprocal viewpoints and gratitude. Only power exercised within the framework of this covenant is legitimate.

On this point I see no differences among Judaism, Christianity, and Islam, and to speak of a separation between the realms of power and authority at this level is to seek to divide the conscience against itself. Any effort to contrast from their moments of origin a Christianity that distinguishes between these realms and an Islam that mixes them would be hasty, superficial, and unacceptable because it would not take account either of historical conditions or of the psychological analysis of the important notion of *debt of meaning*, or even less of the new perspectives opened up by political and religious anthropology.

What has happened historically to the domains of spiritual and temporal power in Christianity? It is not possible here to trace the development of the Byzantine church and the Roman Catholic church up to the great protest of Luther in the sixteenth century. But it is well known that the church sought in every case to supervise imperial and royal power while maintaining its prerogative in the domain of legitimating spiritual authority. The commercial and then capitalist bourgeoisie won its autonomy little by little in the economic sphere and struggled to assign a similar autonomy to the juridical sphere, liberating the state from the religious domain and its ideological nature, which the proponents of the competing bourgeois ideology had come to view as intolerable.

In this confrontation, which I have summarized much too crudely, the line between the symbolic character of religion and secular power became blurred. The symbolic capital carried in religious discourse and practice at the level of the Covenant (*mīthāq*) deteriorated into ritual behavior, legal codes, and monopolies of coercive power exercised by the church in alliance with the state. The rise of a "secular spiritual power"[2] in the bourgeoisie shifted the burden of satisfying the *debt of meaning* from the symbolic capital of the Covenant regime to the institution of universal suffrage. This meant fundamentally that the executions of Charles I and Louis XVI, whatever the faults and political weaknesses of these monarchs, ended a religious symbolism that assured the "functioning"—highly ideological, distorted, and deviant—of the Covenant without there yet being created any resymbolization of the "new covenant" founded on universal suffrage. The exit from religion was brutal, but there remained little islands of religious expression where a more or less blind struggle continued between the church—dragged in spite of itself toward a secularization it could not control—and the state, which was involved more and more in the adventure described by Fernand Braudel as "material civilization."[3]

The functions of myth, symbol, sign, and metaphor in the generation of meaning, and thus of all those systems of significations by which human beings "explain" and "justify" their conduct in society, have been totally neglected and ignored—historically, theologically, philosophically, anthropologically, semiologically—in the historical adventure of the West, both in its exit from traditional religion and its "revolutionary" entry into what Raymond Aron has called secular religions.[4] Under these conditions, churches and states moved closer together again in search of a new set of contracts for a new secularism in order to make possible a new spirituality.

We must look at the case of Islam and the Muslim world in the light of this rapid distillation of the historical trajectory of Christianity and the West. The political and religious situation of Arabia at the beginning of the seventh century differed in essential ways from that of Palestine in the time of Jesus. In Arabia, tribal solidarity permitted the perpetuation of discontinuous, dispersed, rival, mobile political power, which was linked to beliefs, customs, and divinities, all of them different. Clan rivalry affected even Mecca, Yathrib, and Ta'if, the principal towns where the Prophet would undertake his efforts to unify and go beyond precisely those recurrent conflicts dividing and weakening the society. Far from having to work with a strong, organized central authority, Muhammad was obliged to introduce a new political system attuned to a new religious symbolism.

To demand a separation of religious and temporal domains at this early stage in the history of Arabia, characterized by a dispersion of tribes, is to be guilty of anachronism and to ignore the elementary postulates of political and religious anthropology. This is the place to correct the scandalous ignorance of militantly secularist thought. I say *secularist* and not secular because I must remove any possible ambiguity. Open-minded secular thought, applied with a critical perspective to any aspect of knowledge and understood as a search for the most neutral, least ideological form of expression out of respect for the free will of the other person, constitutes significant progress of the mind. I have employed such an approach in teaching at the Sorbonne since 1961, and the intellectual atmosphere of the Sorbonne has helped me to further refine and explore that *responsible* disposition of the mind.

Secularist thought, in contrast, is that which, on the pretext of neutrality, has eliminated from the public schools all scientific instruction in the history of religions understood as a permanent and universal dimension of human societies. The general public has thus become illiterate in all that touches religious life and expression, especially in France. A positivistic, scientistic rationalism[5] has made it impossible for many to even think about the myths, symbols, symbolic capital, and metaphors that have played a decisive role in all religious expression.

As a result, there are still few works that call attention to a simple but paramount historical fact: The activity of the Prophet Muhammad, like that of the biblical prophets who preceded him and that of Jesus himself, consisted in founding a new political order by articulating the religious symbolism of the Covenant. The Prophet fashioned political and religious space at the same time. When he moved the *qibla,* the spiritual orientation toward a sacred place, from Jerusalem to Mecca, when he made Friday the day of collective celebration in imitative rivalry with the symbolism of Sunday and Saturday, when he erected a mosque in Medina and forbade believers to enter a rival mosque, when he came back to Mecca and integrated all the ritual and physical structures of the pagan *ḥajj* ("pilgrimage") into the new Islamic symbolism, when he reworked the rules of inheritance and marriage strategies in a tribal context, he was progressively constructing a semiological system that outmoded that of the former Arab society, outclassed the Jewish, Christian, Sabaean, and Manichean competition, and made possible the edification of a state implementing the new political order. All this was viable because the Qur'an summarized the new religious symbolism in nonsystematic language, permitting the generation of appropriate meanings in even the most changing historical circumstances.

In Islam, as in Christianity and Judaism, symbolism deteriorates into legal codes, mechanical rituals, scholastic doctrines, and ideologies of domination. (I leave aside the cases of the other great religions not to give preference of any kind to the revealed religions but out of a desire for clarity and simplicity.) We can follow this deterioration from the death of the Prophet in 632 and especially after the coming to power of the Umayyads in 661. Historians customarily recount the political events, social changes, and cultural evolution occurring after the foundation of an imperial (Umayyad) state identifying itself with Islam. What they do not sufficiently show is how this Islam became institutionalized as a state to provide centralization and administration of the vast empire put together in exactly the century extending from the death of the Prophet in 632 to the battle of Poitiers in 732, when Charles Martel stopped the Arab-Berber advance coming out of Spain.

The making of Islam into a state signifies the creation of a judicial administration and the elaboration of a legal code that eventually acquired the value of a "religious" law, the *shari'a.* It signifies the spread of a profane culture and civilization—that which the Qur'an called "the world" or "terrestrial life," *al-dunyā*—while the *islām* incarnated by Abraham was being brought together, developed, and interpreted quite differently by the Sufi mystics. The subordination of religion to politics must not be confused with the confounding of the spiritual and the temporal that many criticize today, starting from the concept and development of Western Christianity as described above. Since the death of the Prophet, Islam has never recovered the special circumstances permitting its double expression as symbol and politics: Muhammad put a political order in place by designing immediately and quite adequately a process of symbolization by which every judicial-political decision took its justification and finality from a living relationship with God. This God was not an abstraction or a vision but a living actor, doing and speaking through ritual conduct and exemplary recitation (*qiṣaṣ*), re-evoking for the mythical consciousness the great episodes in salvation history and the sacralizing activities of that time and place in which a small but growing group of believers (*mu'minūn*), actors who today would be called militants, made their mark. Qur'anic discourse faithfully preserves the living memory of this symbolic creativity in a linguistic form declared to be inimitable. It exposes the ethical, legal, and political conduct of believers to a transcendent perspective. (That concept needs to be reworked to take account of the efforts at transcendentalization that occur when the symbolic function deteriorates.) The recurrent force of this transcendence stems very largely from the original link between each verse and a concrete existential situation, either one encountered by the Prophet in developing his experience of the divine or one faced by his community of disciples in their struggle to perpetuate that experience.

The linking of political action to symbolic creativity ended definitively with the rise of the imperial Umayyad state. Instead, there triumphed an inverse process whereby the symbolic capital carried by the Qur'an was utilized for the construction and imposition of an official, orthodox Islam: *official* because it resulted from political choices of the state, which physically eliminated opponents who stood for any other interpretations and uses of the symbolic capital (the Shi'ite and Kharijite protests, most notably); *orthodox* because the experts accredited by the political authorities gave credence to the idea that it is possible to read the Word of God correctly, to know the prophetic tradition exhaustively in order to deduce (*istinbāṭ al-aḥkām*) from the fundamental sources (*uṣūl*) all the legal provisions that constitute the Divine Law (*shari'a*). In this way, during the first two centuries after the Hijra, from roughly 632 to 850, what we call Muslim law (*fiqh*) and legal methods (*uṣūl al-fiqh*) were developed. This legal science was a typically Islamic intellectual effort (*ijtihād*) aimed at sacralizing and transcendentalizing after the fact the *corpus juris* elaborated in the courts, practically speaking, between 632 and about 800.

The notions of sacralization and transcendentalization of a body of law, of a set of public institutions and rules governing the administration of personal matters, and of the role of the caliph are of capital importance if we are to approach correctly the question of Islam and secularism (or secularization). When one speaks of Islam, and I include here Muslims as well as those Orientalists who remain indifferent to the anthropological approach, one immediately invokes an omnipresent, intangible, immobile realm of the sacred and the transcendent. Of course these two notions are changing, relative, and manipulable in every society. Qur'anic discourse has made broad use of them to desacralize the previous Arab pantheon of gods and purge the sacred realm of all the associations made by pagan religion. But nowhere did paganism entirely disappear with the spread of Islam, and the operations of sacralization and transcendentalization thus multiplied and divided, finding support in diverse Qur'anic verses and sayings of the Prophet (hadith). That is why even now there unfolds in all Muslim societies a process that is just the reverse of that which led in the Qur'an to the purification of the sacred and its concentration in the person of God. This same sacred realm has become diffracted and dispersed; it has become incarnated in all the objects and all the works that mediate the divine for believers of diverse cultural and religious origin. An apologetic literature that finds predictions in

the Qur'an of all modern scientific discoveries is one of the recent, significant metamorphoses of this diffraction and of these metaphors of the sacred realm mediated by
Qur'anic verses. The claims that the Prophet and his Companions worked out and
experimented with socialism, democracy, or the proclamation of the rights of man
constitute still other examples.

All this demonstrates that it is illusory to reduce the relationships of religion and
secularism, of the spiritual and the temporal, to a matter of the legal separation of
these realms or to a distinction between theology and philosophy, myth and history.
We must not minimize the importance of the modern separation of legislative, judicial, executive, and spiritual powers for the achievement of social peace and respect
for the rights of all human beings. Nor should we forget that these separate powers all
refer us back to more fundamental questions located *upstream* from all our political,
legal, and religious discourse, questions about being, value, sacredness, transcendence, love, justice, and desire for eternity that motivate our research, inspire our
wars, and promise us satisfactions.

Notes

1. Marcel Gauchet, *Le désenchantement du monde* (Paris: Gallimard, 1982).

2. Paul Benichou, *Le temps des prophètes: doctrines de l'âge romantique* (Paris: Gallimard,
1977); *Morales du grand siècle* (Paris: Gallimard, 1988).

3. See Fernand Braudel, *Afterthoughts on Material Civilization and Capitalism* (Baltimore:
Johns Hopkins, 1977).

4. See Raymond Aron, *L'opium des intellectuels* (Paris: Agora, 1986).

5. See Karl Marx, *Critique of Hegel's Philosophy of Right*, translated by Joseph J. O'Malley
(Cambridge: Cambridge University, 1970).

4

Secularism

Atatürk adopted a neutral position with regard to religion and instituted the Swiss legal code in Turkey. Are these actions to be seen as an isolated phenomenon or as an indication that the Muslim world is evolving toward pluralistic, democratic secularism as did the Christian West?

*T*he case of Turkey and Atatürk (Mustafa Kemal, 1881–1938) merits lengthy analysis because the West often views Turkey with a favorable eye for its audacious charge toward a Western value, secularism. The rest of the Muslim world is thought to have understood nothing of the movement of civilization and to have remained closed off from the progress of ideas and institutions. Such is the intellectual sensitivity with which even Turkey is often perceived in Europe! Tensions erupt periodically in the Council of Europe over this Muslim country, which wishes to be an integral part of Europe, a member of the European Community. In this same line, I would evoke the negative European response to the request of King Hassan II of Morocco, who had the audacity to propose his country for membership in the European Community. Islam clearly continues to constitute today, as it did yesterday, a barrier to communication with the West.

What happened then with Atatürk when he took power after the defeat of Ottoman Turkey, which allied itself with Germany during World War I? Atatürk, considered by his fellow citizens to be a civilizing hero, the father of modern Turkey, without a doubt ripped his country away from Ottoman conservatism and launched it into modernity with a method, convictions, and models that remain highly debatable.

To properly evaluate the range and consequences of his secularizing enterprise it is necessary to answer two questions.[1] With what sort of Islam could Atatürk have been familiar in Turkey between 1881 and 1938, that is to say, during the preparation and development of his program of action? And to what conception of secularism could he have had access in that same period?

Atatürk's views of Islam, on the one hand, and of secularism, on the other, are typical of that naïve state of consciousness found among most Muslim intellectuals between 1880 and 1940. Their passage through European schools and universities had led them to experience a culture shock they never managed to overcome entirely in their later lives. The Muslim society they came from was, in Turkey and elsewhere, gripped by a mass of religious, superstitious, and magic taboos, glaring social inequalities, arbitrary native and colonial policies, and grievous cultural backwardness. All these flaws contrasted violently with Western republican liberties, economic dynamism, cultural creativity, broadness of historical vision, will to know and learn, comfort and cleanliness of public and private areas, development of the land, and the wealth of cities such as Paris, London, Berlin, Brussels, Rome, and Marseille, the great capitals where young Muslims came to study. Atatürk attended the Military Academy of Toulouse in France. His enchantment with discovery became mixed with a blind revolt against an unmerited historical destiny. The Egyptian Tahtawi, and after him Taha Hussein, the Algerian Kateb Yacine, the Tunisian Bourguiba, and so many others have expressed, either in writing or in action, in styles very much their own, their versions of this historic drama that continues to unravel in ever-increasing complexity and on an ever-growing human scale.

Such is the psychocultural background common to all political activity of every Muslim leader at least until the end of World War II. It was the period of naïve consciousness, because these generations believed naïvely that it was enough to take the "prescriptions" for the success of Western civilization and apply them to Muslim countries. Secularism was perceived as one of those effective prescriptions to be applied to societies where religion controlled all the happenings and gestures of daily life. Those generations of Muslim intellectuals did not have a sufficient grasp of history to be able to pin down the ideological genesis, sociopolitical functions, and philosophical limits of secularism in the West. Abdullah Cevet, editor of the Turkish newspaper *Ictihad,* wrote quite naïvely on the eve of Atatürk's revolution: "There is no second civilization; civilization means European civilization, and it must be imported with all its roses and its thorns."

Atatürk went even further, for he was not content to abolish the sultanate, which had been elevated in the collective consciousness to the sacred rank of the caliphate—hence the protest of the ulema of Al-Azhar University in Cairo and the *general* shock to Muslim consciousness. He attacked the semiological universe of Muslims by replacing the Arabic alphabet with the Latin alphabet, the turban and the fez with the hat, and the *shari'a* with the Swiss legal code. Official ceremonies, cooking, furniture, architecture, urbanism, the calendar, all those semiological systems that affect individual and collective sensibilities and control the a priori forms of understanding, were officially abolished and slated for replacement by European systems in the space of a few years. It makes one think of the French revolutionaries who believed they could replace the Christian cult with that of the Supreme Being.

Symbol played a vital role in the construction of a new semantic and semiological order from which the new political, social, juridical order was to be derived. One could, indeed, venture an explication of the durable and recurrent success of traditional religions and the total or partial failure of iconoclastic revolutions by analyzing case by case the manipulation of the symbolic function by prophets and contemporary leaders. Symbol apparently plays a very different role according to whether it is used in the context of a mystically structured oral culture or in the logocentric system of a written culture, enclosed within the boundaries of the historicist view. Atatürk's revolution constituted the triumph of positivist, historicist reason, radically cut off from the mythic consciousness in which the great mass of believers, ulema and illiterate alike, continued to move. The ideological breach between revolutionary leaders and the masses they claimed to emancipate impaired the symbolic capital cultivated by the living tradition. Symbols suddenly became mere signals of recognition for "moderns" and "conservatives." The meaning of these signals was inverted in the anticolonial struggle in Algiers from 1954 to 1962 and in the Islamic revolution in Iran after 1979, when the wearing of the veil by women and of beards and mustaches by men, the multiplication of mosques, and the return to dress, food, and attitudes recommended by the *shari'a* meant political resistance against illegitimate states—colonial in the case of Algeria and secular in the case of the shah's Iran; after victory, the same signals referred to the expression of national-religious identities.

To write in this way about the history of contemporary "Islam," not on the level of political events and with the ideological vocabulary of nationalist historiography but at the level of anthropological structures of the imaginary, where symbol deteriorates into sign and signal, and where signal tries in vain to recover symbolic function, is to *rethink* the destiny of all societies in a radically new field of intelligibility. Current scientific culture permits us to glimpse opportunity for such a cognitive leap, which would serve to demystify many a murderous leader and "revolution," but the schools and universities directly tied to the political viewpoint of these leaders are not yet ready to diffuse this new scientific spirit.

The example of Turkey, profoundly marked by the work of Atatürk, is particularly fertile ground to study the degradation of symbols into signals and the effort to bring signals back toward symbols in an ideological and cultural context that provokes reflection, as well, on the irreversibility of the history of societies. In the case of Turkey, the weight of Islam interferes more heavily than ever with the availability of the country for Europeanization. All Muslims who care about enriching contemporary Islamic thought must spend time examining the Turkish example.

Thus, two subjects that obsess all Muslim societies and relate directly to Atatürk's iconoclastic experiment must be studied by those with anthropological training. I am speaking first of what Arabs call the *turāth,* the cultural heritage of the classical period of Muslim history (632–1258), and second of *al-ghazw al-fikrī,* the cultural assault of the West exemplified by the work of Atatürk. The repercussions of this assault have not yet played themselves out.

Notes

1. See my article "Positivism et tradition dans une perspective islamique," *Diogène* 127 (July-September 1984).

✵ 5 ✵

Nationalism

How has the nationalist model worked in Muslim societies since the attainment of independence?

*L*ike secularism, nationalism is an example of the historical and semantic deterioration of a symbolic universe into a collection of signals operating in contemporary societies. Indeed, the nationalist model was borrowed from national movements as they developed in European countries in the nineteenth century. Each newly independent Muslim country needed desperately to establish a government capable of managing not only the problems inherited from colonialism but also the global historical destiny of the society, taking into account the "identity" demanded by its inhabitants and the categorical imperative of modern economic development. These tasks—multiple, heavy, old, and new—are in any case difficult to circumscribe and to identify with an eye to appropriate political action.

It is impossible to provide a global analysis that would be valid for all Muslim societies from Indonesia, colonized by the Netherlands; to Pakistan, which detached itself from India to form a Muslim nation; Morocco, which had lived continuously under an Islamic state from the foundation of the Idrisid dynasty in 808 until the establishment of the French protectorate in 1904; and Algeria, where, contrary to nationalist affirmations, the state had been a discontinuous institution in space and time before the French conquest starting in 1832. One could continue this list and indicate distinguishing features of each case at the level of typology of states and national "unity."

I will, however, introduce only a basic distinction between the countries affected by colonization, such as Algeria, Tunisia, and Morocco; those that underwent political tutelage, such as Iran, Iraq, and Yemen; and those that preserved relative independence, such as Turkey and most of Arabia. Two historic events that have in differing degrees conditioned the operation of the nationalist model since independence should also be kept in mind. The first such event was the brutal interruption of the Sunni caliphate with the entry of Mongol invaders into Baghdad in 1258. Sunnis perceived the caliphate as the vicariate of the Prophet, though with less charismatic stature than that recognized in the designated imams by Twelver and Ismaili Shi'a. To be sure, the caliphate had been little more than a legal and religious fiction since 945, when the Buyids took over real power in Baghdad and Rajj. Likewise, the Fatimid Imamate at Mahdiyya in Tunisia and later in Cairo had been brilliant but ephemeral

(909–1171). The Ottomans tried to revive the caliphate in an effort to exercise centralized authority over the *dār al-islām,* but they never dared resume use of the title "caliph," much less that of "imam." They settled for the sultanate, which Atatürk abolished in 1923. The Ottoman failure was the second event that conditioned the nationalist model.

The caliphate and the imamate, like the Ottoman sultanate, presupposed a political space once called *mamlaka* ("kingdom" or "empire"), which was legally and theologically defined as the *dār al-islām* (the "house" or "territory" of Islam). The Muslim subjects recognizing this central authority formed the *umma* ("community"), an entity whose essence was religious, because its members were bound by a spiritual brotherhood that the caliph, the imam, or the "legitimate" sultan was to protect. The consciousness of the *umma* was essentially mythical. It fed on the sacred presence of a "spiritual" leader insofar as he correctly fulfilled his role as vicar of the Prophet. That means he had no legislative power and that he was obliged to insure the strict application of the "objective" law, that of God, which had been revealed to the Prophets, fleshed out in detail by God himself, transmitted scrupulously by the Companions, developed by the legal-scholar/theologians, and applied with a technique excluding any personal adaptation by the judges (qadis).

Potentially and theologically all members of the *umma* participate in this politico-religious system. Ethnoculturally and sociologically, the *mamlaka,* the lands and countries possessed by the centralized "Muslim" state, covered such a diversity of cultures and ethnic groups that many of them remained and remain today outside the political, legal, and cultural control of the caliphate, imamate, or sultanate. Algeria under Ottoman rule exemplified this situation, as did Morocco in the nineteenth century, when the country was split into *blād al-makhzan* and *blād al-siba,* the territory controlled by the state and the territory of rebellion.

All those states formed after independence came to mistrust ethnological and anthropological research, which they rejected as "colonial" science. To build national unity on a territorial base defined by what are now international boundaries, one must avoid the awakening of cultural and linguistic identities that might be tempted to utilize the same nationalist claims once directed against the foreign colonial power. The genesis of national unity in France, Italy, Spain, and Germany encountered the same tensions, the same contradictions. We are familiar with the nationalist rigor of the French Jacobin model, which all the states of the Third World emerging from colonial struggle adopted, with even greater determination to centralize than the Jacobins themselves had demonstrated.

Deprived of institutional references in an "Islamic" past abolished long ago, fascinated by the power and efficacy of national models like those of France, Italy, and England, the contemporary Muslim states have improvised in nation building without regard for the institutional void left by the history of the caliphate-imamate-sultanate, for the legitimate expectations of ethnocultural groups driven back into vestigiality and marginality, for the excesses and negative consequences of the Jacobin model, or for the political philosophy inspiring the federal model.

The interests of political leaders and intellectual elites converged in imposing the nationalist Jacobin model and beating back any corrective, whether from history, sociology, anthropology, political philosophy, or legal criticism. All these disciplines are still little encouraged in the all-too-young universities of Muslim countries. What is more, the state always draws the most visible intellectuals into intellectual solidarity with policies adopted by the single party, the president, or the king. During the Nasserist period, intellectuals of great renown were found to defend not just the nations being built inside each country but also the great Arab nation, of which Colonel Qadhdhafi remains the faithful partisan today.

Similarly, Maghribi leaders periodically invoke the building of a great Arab Maghrib when internal problems make it necessary to open transnational horizons for the powerful echoes in popular consciousness they produce. It is the same with the aspirations for the unity of the *umma,* which neither the Islamic Conference Organization nor the World Islamic League manages to make credible. All this shows that the nations under construction are still in the stage of tests, improvisations, and decisions taken at the top. However, these peoples possess a wealth of resources still poorly understood, poorly interpreted, and insufficiently exploited. In vain they request means of democratic expression; explosions of anger are quickly repressed, dismissed as "betrayal" of the national cause, or cleverly recycled for other purposes by authorities interested only in assuring their own survival. I would not be surprised if these reflections, however moderate and well supported, elicited retaliation by "authentic" militants or by "orthodox" defenders of national unity. In the end, genuine unity must result from the freely expressed will of all citizens, but the path that leads there remains long, muddy, and disconcerting.

6

Revelation

Islam is based on a book of revelation, the Qur'an. What is meant by "revelation," and what does the word "Qur'an" mean?

Let's begin with the meaning of the word "Qur'an," a participle of the word *qara'a*, "to read." In the word "Qur'an" itself, the root *q-r-'* has the sense of reciting more than of reading, for it does not presuppose the existence of a written text when Muhammad first enunciated his revelation. Thus verses 16 and 17 of Sura 75 say: "Don't move your tongue to recite [the Qur'an] as if you wanted to hurry with the enunciation. It falls to us to put it together and proclaim it [*qur'ānahu*]; and when we have proclaimed it, to recite it faithfully; then it is our task to make it clear."

Several verses emphasize the Prophet's need to conform to the enunciation of verses according to the *recitation* as he heard them. Orientalist philologists suggest that the word *qur'ān* has Syriac or Hebraic origins, but this observation does not modify the meaning required by the Qur'anic context itself. The principal idea is that of a recitation conforming to a discourse that is heard, not read. That is why I prefer to speak of Qur'anic *discourse* and not of *text* in the initial phase of enunciation by the Prophet. The putting into writing of the whole of the revealed discourse comes under the reign of the third caliph, 'Uthman, between 645 and 656. The distinction between speech and text takes on an even greater importance in the light of modern linguistics.[1]

The Qur'an bears other names, such as *al-kitāb*, the Book, the writings "descended" from the sky in the course of the "Blessed Night"; *al-dhikr*, "the warning" (and thus the peoples of the Book, *ahl al-kitāb*, are also called *ahl al-dhikr*, those people who have received the warning or who cause the names of God and his teachings to be remembered); *al-furqān*, "the discrimination" or the discriminating proof, that is to say, the revelation.[2]

The question of revelation is more delicate, especially if one wishes to get beyond and renew "orthodox" teachings piously repeated within each of the monotheistic traditions. It is not a matter of ignoring or overturning these teachings; the science of religions today seeks rather to understand the theological and historical genesis of them, their ideological and psychological functions, their semantic and anthropological limits and inadequacies. It would take too long here to do such analysis and provide this kind of an account. I will, instead, emphasize lines of research that, by avoiding all dogmatic definitions, would make possible the understanding of revelation as a linguistic and cultural phenomenon prior to any effort at constructing a theology upon it.

The Islamic conception of revelation is called *tanzīl* ("descent"), a fundamental metaphor for the vertical gaze human beings are invited to cast toward God, transcendence. *Tanzīl* refers to the object of a revelation; the Qur'an speaks also of *wahy*, which is the very act of revelation by God to the prophets. Here is how the Qur'an details the mechanisms of *wahy* in Sura 42, verse 51/52:

> Man is not of a dignity such that God speaks to him other than by means of *wahy* or from behind a veil or by sending him a Messenger who, with the permission of God, communicates the *wahy* that God wants to give him. God is Transcendent and Wise.
>
> It is thus that we have sent a breath of life (*rūh*), acting on Our Orders; you did not know that it was neither the Book nor the Faith; we have made a Light by which We guide those whom We wish among Our servants. And you, in truth, lead with certainty toward the Straight Path.

In the following sura, number 43, verses 1–5, the Qur'an offers further details:

> Ha. Mim. By the clarifying Book! Yes, We have made an Arab Qur'an so that you can perhaps recognize [the signs of an eternal Message].
>
> And, in truth, this Qur'an is an integral part of the Archetype of the Book [*umm al-kitāb*], which is there in Our Presence, Transcendent and all Wisdom.
>
> Will we give up on reminding you of the Message [*al-dhikr*] by virtue of the fact that you as a people have sinned to excess?

The vocabulary of revelation used by the Qur'an itself is difficult to translate into our desacralized languages, cut off from the system of connotations relevant to religious discourse in the Semitic languages. That is why I have not translated the key term, *wahy*. Exegetists speak of an inspiration putting itself forward, either as a suggestion solicited by God in the spirit of a human being to permit him to understand the substance of the Message, or as an enunciation articulated in human language and communicated to the prophets, directly or with the mediation of an angel. The term *qur'ān* thus takes on the meaning of recitation. Similarly, *rūh*, which stands properly for the breath of life, is interpreted as the spirit carried by the revelation or the angel carrying revelation. The notion of the Archetype of the Book, transcendent, replete with wisdom, and kept in the presence of God, is also essential to defining accurately the status of the Qur'an, understood as enunciations articulated in Arabic to explain clearly to human beings the truths and commandments of which God chooses to remind sinful peoples, as he already had with the prophets before Muhammad.

These definitions, which no Muslim can dispute, permit me to sketch the first move toward a comparative theology of revelation. Whereas Jews and Muslims concur comfortably that God reveals his will to human beings via the mediation of prophets (with the difference that Muslims recognize all the prophets of Israel, while the Jews have always refused to accord Muhammad this status), Christians stake a claim irreducibly different from the Judeo-Islamic position: Jesus Christ, they say, is the Word of God become flesh. He is the incarnation of God, the son of God come to live among men in order to communicate directly, without the mediation of an angel or a prophet, the Divine Word. In this conception, the New Testament is only an account of what the disciples heard and remembered of the teaching of the Son of God, speaking in the name of the Father.

Let's leave aside the formidable question of the Trinity, which can be discussed usefully among Christians, Jews, and Muslims only if, going behind dogmatic definitions handed down in each tradition, we agree on the semantic status of metaphor and symbol in the structure of meaning in naturally occurring languages. The problem is linguistic more than it is theological. We do not yet possess a theory of metaphor and symbol that would permit us to take account of the strictly linguistic genesis of meaning *and* of the philosophical status of the meaning thus engendered. The arbitrariness of traditional theological definitions resides in the fact that they presuppose a solution to the problem of metaphor and symbol in religious discourse. Metaphor adds an aesthetic ornament to a discourse that refers directly to objects, substances, and mental entities called by names that God himself has taught us, according to a biblical verse echoed in the Qur'an and supported at a linguistic level by classical philology. With a philosophy of language such as that perpetuated by theological teaching, the successive revelations are *substantialized,* essentialized, frozen in denotations belonging to the system of signs that conditions the lexicological and semantic operation of each language. The grammarian Al-Sirafi and the logician Matta Ibn Yunus raised and discussed this problem clearly within the tradition of Arab thought in the tenth century.[3]

It is clear that any modern reinterpretation of the notion of revelation will depend on solutions to the initial linguistic and logical problems of nomenclature in naturally occurring languages. Without prejudging what these solutions might turn out to be, we can open a common field of endeavor for the three traditions of theological research by using the Qur'anic distinction between the Archetype of the Book and the Arabic-language Qur'an.

Would Christian theology be willing to say that the discourse of Jesus Christ in Aramaic (and not Greek; the distinction is important) at a precise time and in a precise place on Earth is related to God the Father as the Qur'anic discourse in Arabic transmitted by Muhammad is related to the Archetype of the Book retained in the presence of God transcendent?

Even if this analogy brought objections from one side or the other, no one—not Christians, not Jews, not Muslims—can escape the following historical, linguistic, and cultural constraint: The messages transmitted by the prophets of Israel, Jesus Christ, and Muhammad were first oral enunciations, heard and memorized by disciples who subsequently acted as witnesses and transmitters of that which they heard and saw. In each case, whatever the theological status of the first enunciation of the message, there was a passing to a *text,* a fixing in writing of the message put together in historical conditions that must be, and already have more or less satisfactorily been, an object of scrutiny for the historian.

The texts constituted in this fashion, the Old Testament, the New Testament, the *muṣḥaf* (i.e., the book composed of pages where the Qur'anic discourse is transcribed), were elevated to the status of a Closed Official Corpus according to procedures developed and supervised by scholars: *official* because they resulted from a set of decisions taken by "authorities" recognized by the community; *closed* because nobody was permitted any longer to add or subtract a word, to modify a reading in the Corpus now declared authentic. Then, in a decisive, irreversible, historic event shared by the three interrelated religious tendencies, revelation came to be accessible to the faithful only on the basis of the Closed Official Corpus, more commonly called Holy Scripture or the Word of God. Here must, however, be noted an important difference between Jews and Muslims, who continue to use the language of the original enunciations, and Christians, who abandoned Aramaic for Greek, Latin, and various national languages after the sixteenth century.

The substitution of texts for oral discourse engendered two phenomena of great cultural and historical ramification. It put the peoples of the Book in a hermeneutic position; that is to say, they needed to *interpret* the holy texts to derive law, prescriptions, and systems of belief and nonbelief of the sort that dominated the moral, legal, and political order until the triumph of secularization. (As indicated above, a breakdown of the order came with the English and French revolutions, but nowhere did the breakdown bring about the complete elimination of the hermeneutic condition.) It also banalized the Holy Book by putting it within the reach of everyone, particularly after the invention of paper and then the printing press. The development of the book as an instrument of culture and a vehicle of civilization contributed to the circulation of the Book as the receptacle of revelation and the diffusion of other books derived from it, such as those of exegesis, theology, law, professions of faith, catechism, and translation. It is in this sense that I speak of societies of the Book/book, where the Holy Book continues to shape and direct the production of books and, as a result, the knowledge business as a whole in highly secularized societies. Inversely, the cultural growth of the Holy Book drew it into history and progressively stripped away its transcendence. This interaction between the Book and books has remained an essential characteristic of societies where the legitimacy of the state was tied or is still tied to the phenomenon of the Book, referring to revelation. That is why a history of these societies must integrate this dimension into a global reconstruction of their mechanisms of development rather than detaching religion from other factors producing each society. Further on I will show how social actors have continuously sought help from the Book to sacralize or transcendentalize their conduct, works, values, even the most profane of their visions. I emphasize this function of the Book because it has become dominant and unmistakable to the point of being intolerable in contemporary Muslim societies. Let's not forget, however, that the separation of religious and temporal domains in Western societies screens the ever-functioning mechanisms of the societies of the Book/book from the eyes of the observer.

John Paul II contributed mightily to popularizing the religious phenomenon once again, in the light of increasing disaffection with ideologies that had since the nineteenth century been working actively to install scientific socialism. The competition is still on; societies of the Book/book, like socialist or liberal societies, require fresh analysis with new scientific equipment.

Taking into consideration all the experiments generated in the societies of the Book/book, one could say it is a revelation each time that a new vocabulary comes to radically change man's view of his condition, his *being-in-the-world*, his participation in the production of meaning. Revelation is the accession to the interior space of a human being—to the heart, the *qalb,* says the Qur'an—of some novel meaning that opens up unlimited opportunities or backcurrents of meaning for human existence.

The revelations collected in the Old Testament, the New Testament, and the Qur'an fit easily within this definition. They should not be confused with theological systems, exegeses, or legal codes that managers of the sacred establishments have drawn from them at various times. These derivatives constitute some among many meanings potentially contained in revelation. Revelation feeds a living tradition that permits the community to resupply itself periodically with the radical novelty of the original message; all the while sacralization and transcendentalization are tending to pervert and freeze the liberating vista of revelation.

As examples of the dynamic operation of revelation in history, I would cite the experience of exile in Judaism, redemption in Christianity, and *hijra* ("migration") toward the absoluteness of God in Islam. Enough has been said on these themes within the three communities that we need not be detained by them here. The liberating vista of these three crowning events is obvious enough to justify our distinction between the revealing and transforming power of revelation and the repetitive behavior that social actors deduce from it.

This definition of revelation has the merit of making a place for the teachings of Buddha, Confucius, African elders, and all the great voices that recapitulate the collective experience of a group in order to project it toward new horizons and enrich the human experience of the divine. We manage thus to guide ourselves toward another variety of religious thought and go beyond all previous experience with the sacred.

Notes

1. See my *Lectures du Coran* (Paris: Maisonneuve et Larose, 1982), chap. 1.

2. See the *Encyclopedia of Islam,* 2nd ed., under these words.

3. See Djamäl Al Amrani, *Logique aristotélicienne et grammaire arabe (études et documents)* (Paris: J. Vrin, 1983); see also my *Humanisme arabe au IVᵉ/IXᵉ siècle,* 2nd ed. (Paris: J. Vrin, 1982), p. 189.

🐾 7 🐾

The Qur'an

When was the Qur'an written and by whom? What does this book contain?

*I*n the preceding pages I have offered partial responses to these questions, but I want to come back to the question of oral and written messages to look at them more rigorously from an anthropological viewpoint. In this way I hope to shed greater light not only on the question of the Qur'an, transformed into *mushaf,* but also on the more general issues of meaning in the conflict between societies without writing and societies of the Book/book.

According to Muslim tradition, the assembling of the Qur'an began at the death of the Prophet in 632, but even while he was alive it seems that certain verses were put into writing. Partial compilations were made with rather unsatisfactory materials, for paper was not yet known to the Arabs and would not be available to them until nearly the end of the eighth century. The dying off of the Companions of the Prophet, those who had journeyed with him from Mecca to Medina in 622, and a sharpening of debate among surviving Muslims pushed the third caliph, 'Uthman, to gather the totality of the revelation into a single compilation called *mushaf.* The collection was declared complete, finished, and closed; the text was established *ne varietur;* and the partial compilations were destroyed to avoid feeding dissent about the authenticity of the revelations selected. This process of selection and destruction necessitates our recourse to the notion of Closed Official Corpus.

Modern historians have examined this question with critical rigor, principally because the Qur'an was assembled in a very troubled political climate. A German Arabist carried out the first critical examination of the story of the Qur'anic text in about 1860.[1] A French scholar tried to refine this research by proposing a chronological order for the suras, an issue that had preoccupied Muslim jurists seeking to identify which verses abrogated others and which were abrogated by others (*al-nāsikh wal-mansūkh*).[2]

It is unfortunate that philosophical critique of sacred texts—which has been applied to the Hebrew Bible and to the New Testament without thereby engendering negative consequences for the notion of revelation—continues to be rejected by Muslim scholarly opinion. The works of the German school continue to be ignored, and erudite Muslims do not dare draw upon such research even though it would serve to strengthen the scientific foundations of the history of the *mushaf* and of the theology of revelation. The reasons for this resistance are political and psychological.

Politically, in the absence of democratic mechanisms, the Qur'an plays an indispensable role in the process of legitimation in the new states. Psychologically, ever since the failure of the Mu'tazili school to impose its view of the Qur'an (*mushaf*) as created by God in time,[3] Muslim consciousness has incorporated the belief that all the pages bound together as *mushaf* contain the very Word of God. The written Qur'an thus has become identified with the Qur'anic discourse or the Qur'an as it was recited, which is itself the direct emanation of the Archetype of the Book.

This means that the phenomenon of writing as a means of transition to a different functioning of language and as an archival base linked to state authority is denied in the name of a theological position contradicted by numerous and explicit Qur'anic verses. We know that the Arab orthography evolved quickly with the growth of the Umayyad state. A functional solidarity emerged among the state, the written word, the learned culture of the bureaucrats and clerks in the service of the state, and religious orthodoxy as defined by the jurist-theologians recognized by the state. This solidarity developed at the expense of a rival solidarity that the centralizing state, in the name of the revealed truth it controlled, sought to overcome: the solidarity of segmentary society (tribes, clans, patriarchal families), oral culture, and heterodoxy, or popular religions. Already the Qur'an bore traces of the struggle against this second kind of solidarity in its denunciations of those of the *jāhiliyya*, or gentiles, polytheists (*mushrikūn*), hypocrites (*munāfiqūn*), and bedouins (*a'rāb*). In the place of "shadows" (*zulumāt*), ignorance, and the arbitrary customs and beliefs of former times (*ṭāghūt, asāṭīr al-awwalīn*), the Qur'an put true and enlightening knowledge (*'ilm*) as it was preserved in the "book," understood as the written message, the Just Law, the accounts (*qiṣaṣ*) recapitulating salvation history, and the eternal Covenant between God and human beings within which all political and juridical pacts (*'ahd*) for the earthly city must be concluded.

The distinction introduced by the Qur'an and translated politically by the state, juridically by the *shari'a,* and theologically by professions of faith (*'aqīda*) is of anthropological importance. In the whole Islamic domain since the triumph of the model state in Medina, this sort of solidarity based on politics, law, and theology has fought, rejected, marginalized, and eliminated, if possible, the second, alternative kind of solidarity. Conversely, segmentary society has been able to obstruct and weaken the state, as Ibn Khaldun saw quite correctly.[4] And in this recurrent rivalry between the domain of the state (*blād al-makhzan*) and the domain of rebellion (*blād al-siba*), in the official terminology used in Morocco in the nineteenth century, the omnipresence of the *mushaf* has sanctified the written word in the collective consciousness, which in turn has been an effective instrument of power. It goes without saying that the situation described here for the Islamic example is valid for all Christianity and, what is more, for the imperial West as it transmits its models to societies without a written language, just as contemporary "Muslim" states do for minority groups whose "dialects" are not written.

To look at the "Holy Scriptures" from this historical, sociological, and anthropological angle is obviously to challenge all sacralizing and transcendentalizing interpre-

tations produced by traditional theological reasoning. This process of demystifica-
tion and demythologization of the phenomenon of the Book/book occurs inevitably
today; in fact, many societies have experienced this process for centuries without being able to tame it. I do not mean a kind of demythologization that would reduce
myth to an object of rationalist, historicist, and positivist knowledge.[5] Modern rationality restores the psychological and cultural functions of myth and develops a global
strategy of knowledge in which the rational and the imaginary interact perpetually to
produce individual and historical existence. We must abandon the dualist framework
of knowledge that pits reason against imagination, history against myth, true against
false, good against evil, and reason against faith. We must postulate a plural, changing, welcoming sort of rationality, one consistent with the psychological operations
that the Qur'an locates in the heart and that contemporary anthropology attempts to
reintroduce under the label of the imaginary.

Let's come back again to *mushaf* to clarify a situation that popular theology, in the
form of Ash'arism, Hanbalism, and Ishraqism,[6] has utterly obscured ever since the
early centuries of Islam. By a series of confusions characteristic of the operation of the
religious imaginary (and in a broad sense, of the political realm, which contrary to
the claims of secularist ideology is inseparable from it), the values and irreducible
functions characteristic of (1) the Archetype of the Book, (2) Qur'anic discourse, (3)
the Closed Official Corpus, and (4) the body of interpretative work were projected
into the *mushaf*.[7] The *mushaf* became an object of infinite interpretation aimed at all
believers, and ideologies were constructed to replace theology and "orthodox" truths.

The levels of signification and functioning of that which we commonly and very
generally call the Qur'an can be described and represented in diagrammatic form (see
Figure 7.1). In this figure, I have portrayed the movement by which God revealed a
part of the Heavenly Book to human beings on the vertical axis, symbolic of the "descent" of revelation and the climb back toward transcendence. On the horizontal
axis, that of earthly history, the *human* operations lead from the Qur'anic discourse
(oral pronouncements by the Prophet at moments of opportunity, *asbab al-nuzul*,
not all of which were faithfully reported) to the Closed Official Corpus and then on
to the Corpus of Interpretation, that is to say, the numerous commentaries written
by a most diverse set of commentators. These commentators sought to elaborate on
revealed truths to illuminate the conduct of human beings through the course of
earthly history in the world down here (*al-dunya*). This earthly history is thus entirely lived as a passage toward the Other World (*al-akhira*) after the test of Resurrection and Last Judgment. Human beings return in this fashion to God, conforming to
the plan revealed in the Qur'an.

All these meanderings, all these mental and cultural exercises, and all these images
depend on the *mushaf* for their concrete references and their field of projection. The
mushaf is the volume I as a believer touch, carry, read, and interpret after performing
ritual purification ablutions (*la yamussuhu illa-l-mutahharun*); the sense of the divine
that shapes and moves religious consciousness cannot do without a material vehicle.
Lacking the application of critical analysis, the imaginary absorbs unhindered the

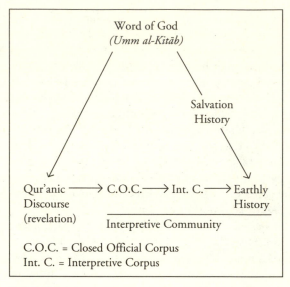

FIGURE 7.1

images that come to constitute a system of plausible truths. In this fashion, consensuses of the Community emerge over time to enrich the living "orthodox" tradition. I am thinking, for example, about the reception given to certain interpretative works such as those of al-Tabari, which were ultimately identified with the contents of the *mushaf*—that is to say, with the "Qur'an" understood as that space where the levels distinguished in Figure 7.1 come together.

The psychocultural preeminence of the physical book where the discourse of revelation has been stored is confirmed by Byzantine iconography representing Christ in his majesty upon a magnificent throne (*'arsh* in the Qur'an). With his right hand he gives blessing and in his left he holds an open copy of the New Testament.[8]

Taking account of all this analysis, one must admit that it is difficult to describe the contents of the Qur'an. In trying to do so one risks falling instantly into the style of the Interpretive Corpus, thus contributing to the traditional religious imaginary. Moreover, the order of appearance of suras and verses in the *mushaf* does not reflect either chronological or rational, formal criteria. With minds accustomed to a rhetoric of composition and a method of exposition that must project an "argument," Western readers are surprised by the "disorder" of the *mushaf* text.

"Disorder" conceals a profound semiotic order and points up the need to distinguish the types of discourse utilized in the Qur'an. I distinguish five:[9] prophetic, legislative, narrative, sapiential, and hymnal (poetic). The contents and levels of signification of these types of discourse can be easily differentiated, but they all proclaim a revelatory purpose, since the totality of Qur'anic discourse follows the same structure of grammatical relations concerning the person: A divine *I/We* addresses with the imperative mode (*qul,* or "say," "speak") an intermediary *you* (Muhammad) to reach the *they* of human beings subdivided into *you,* believers, and *they,* infidels. Such is the realm of grammatical communication defined in all Qur'anic discourse. Inside that realm, pronouncements with profane content, such as laws on inheritance and the prescription of lawful levels of giving to the poor (*zakāt*), are bound together simultaneously in the divine domain of the *I/We* speaker-sender and recipient *you.* There exist thematic and conceptual analyses of the Qur'an, but they do not manage to treat exhaustively the network of connections established within the vocabulary, which is highly recurrent but constantly enriched by the creation of metaphor, symbol, and myth (which is different from mythology). In that area lies a very productive field for research in the pursuit of a modern theory of religious discourse, which is itself a necessary precondition for the construction of any theology liberated from traditional dogmas.

The practical and existential reading of the Qur'an by Muslims over the past 1,300 years constitutes an immense data bank for a phenomenology of a religious consciousness fed by a text that it constantly reworks. This text never ceases to produce, with changing procedures and strategies, secondary, integrating texts where all the cultures of "Islam" exert their influence. And there lies another fascinating, but as yet scarcely touched, field of investigation: the Qur'anic text taken as a part of a very tangled intertextuality. This concept of intertextuality refers in literary criticism to all the texts explicitly or implicitly linked to a poem, a novel, a short story, or a philosophical essay. In the case of the Qur'an, historians have demonstrated links with the Hebrew Bible, the Gospels, ancient Middle Eastern literature such as the story of Alexander the Great, the Gilgamesh legend, and the Seven Sleepers of Ephesus.[10]

The exploration of this vast, interrelated literature helps to show the continuity and creativity of a religious-literary imaginary common to Middle Eastern culture. The Qur'an belongs to this culture and this powerful, expansive imaginary. The dynamic perspective opened by the concept of intertextuality leads to an understanding of religious literature that is richer than the linear reading long required by the philological search for lexical, stylistic, and thematic influences.

There is pressing need to analyze the relevance of the readings already done on the Hebrew Bible, the Gospels, and the Qur'an as examples of a more general linguistic phenomenon, religious discourse. Historians, semioticians, philologists, and literary critics have thus far worked separately on fragments of each great corpus. Lacking are cross-textual and methodological studies devoted not only to each corpus taken as a whole, as it has been read and used through the centuries by each community of believers, but to the three main "holy" books, articulated with the same linguistic, semiotic tools and using the same basic mythical knowledge to generate an axiological discourse called revelation. The relationship between religiously oriented readings and the purely "scientific," nontheistic, nonspiritual, and nonaxiological research must be recognized and assessed.

Notes

1. Th. Nöldeke, *Geschichte des Qorans,* 1st ed., 1860; 2nd ed., Schwally, 1909; 3rd ed., Bergsträsser-Pretzl, 1926–1935.

2. Régis Blachère, *Le Coran: traduction selon un essai de reclassement des sourates* (Paris: Maisonneuve, 1947).

3. By putting the Qur'an within history, the Mu'tazili opened it to discussion and to the "rationalism" for which Mu'tazili scholars were known. A few Abbasid caliphs found political advantage in the position and adopted it, partly to free themselves from the strictures imposed by mainstream ulema claiming to be the authorized interpreters of a Closed Official Corpus beyond the realm of debate and change. See the discussion of the ethical consequences of the Mu'tazili position in Arkoun's *L'Islam, morale et politique* (Paris: Desclée de Brouwer, 1986), pp. 99–102.—TRANS.

4. Ibn Khaldun, *The Muqaddima,* translated by Franz Rosenthal, 2nd ed. (Princeton: Princeton University, 1967).

5. Rudolf Bultmann, *History and Eschatology* (Edinburgh: Edinburgh University, 1975).

6. Henri Corbin, *En Islam iranien: aspects spirituels et philosophiques,* 4 vols. (Paris: Gallimard, 1971–1972).

7. *Mushaf* is a theological concept by which the text of the Qur'an is considered the unobjectionable, unthought, underived Word of God. It is seen to have emerged without the application of human effort or methodologies.

8. See Leonid Ouspensky and Vladimir Lossky, *The Meaning of Icons,* edited and translated by G. E. Palmer and E. Kadbloubovsky, rev. ed. (Crestwood, N.Y.: St. Vladimir's, 1982), p. 71.

9. I use the typology proposed by Paul Ricoeur for the Bible. See *La Révélation,* Ricoeur with Emmanuel Levinas and Edgar Haulotte (Brussels: Facultés St. Louis, 1977).

10. See my study of Sura 18 in *Lectures du Coran* (Paris: Maisonneuve et Larose, 1982; 2nd ed., Tunis, 1991).

❧ 8 ❧

Exegesis

What sort of exegesis was done on this text once it became a book?

There does not yet exist any exhaustive history of Qur'anic exegesis (*tafsīr*) that could speak to two concerns:

1. Defining the genesis, kinship, and historic diversification of a rather large literature, with special attention to the beginnings. Many partial studies seek to satisfy this thrust of curiosity, but as an example of what remains to be done, suffice it to say that the great *tafsīr* of al-Tabari, who died in 923, has not yet been the subject of a scientific study worthy of his place in the history of exegesis. This lacuna suggests that Muslims prefer to "consume" the Qur'an in their daily lives rather than see it subjected to modern scientific examination. In fact, another great *tafsīr* done by a Sunni authority, Fakhr al-din al-Razi, who died in 1209, also awaits scientific treatment.

2. Studying the conditions for the exercise of Islamic reason in each ancient or contemporary commentary. It is indeed essential to show how the theological, historical, and linguistic postulates of this reasoning have led to confusion about levels of signification in the Qur'an. I undertook such a demonstration in two books, *Readings of the Qur'an* (I insist on the plural) and *Toward a Critique of Islamic Reason.*[1] This sort of work is imperative for the definition or redefinition of the theoretical conditions for any "reading" of the Qur'an in the current linguistic sense of that term, which is not to be confused with the readings or textual variations reported within the tradition after the establishment of the *mushaf.* The "readings," *qirā'āt,* selected within the tradition come from either seven or fourteen chains of authorities and are themselves declared "orthodox" and complete.

Classic exegesis knew nothing, of course, of modern textual linguistics and interpretive theory. Al-Tabari could naïvely introduce each of his commentaries with the formula "God says ... ," *yaqūlu allah,* postulating implicitly the perfect equation of exegesis with the intended meaning and, of course, with the semantic content of the words in each verse. Contemporary exegesis has obviously not been delivered from such naïveté; quite to the contrary, the increased literacy of the masses, the broader distribution of books, and the new opportunity to write for newspapers and magazines has put exegesis within the reach of everyone. As a result, we see a degradation of the standards of knowledge maintained by the classical practitioners. The linguistic introductions to classic works of *uṣūl al-fiqh* demonstrate a sharp, clear consciousness of the linguistic conditions for exegesis of any sort.

Contemporary exegesis offers another example of the semantic disorder and dangerous confusion about the Qur'an and what can be deduced from it in the current context of ideologies of liberation. This kind of exegesis leads one to forget the primary function of revelation: to reveal meanings without reducing the mystery, the inexpressible character, of that which is revealed; to show without demonstrating and without short-circuiting the tools of knowledge; in short, to institute a relation of human beings to God that is not one of question and response but consists in playing host to a power equipped with an infinite capacity to signify things, including the truth of being. For the classical practitioners, the authenticity of their religious experience compensated for the inadequacy of their exegesis; contemporary militants have distanced themselves both from the divine and from the conditions for playing host to the divine-revealing word.

Notes

1. Mohammed Arkoun, *Lectures du Coran* (Paris: Maisonneuve et Larose, 1982; 2nd ed., Tunis, 1991); *Pour une critique de la raison islamique* (Paris: Maisonneuve et Larose, 1984).

🌿 9 🌿

Muhammad

What did Muhammad want?

$\mathcal{T}$o approach the person and personality of Muhammad[1] is as difficult and contro-versial as to treat the Qur'an itself. The divergence of Muslim and Orientalist atti-tudes toward Muhammad is as blatant as it is toward the history of the Qur'anic text or the formation of Muslim law (*fiqh*). Just as Muslims continue to foster a hagio-graphic literature often bubbly in its piety, Orientalists are fervently intent on apply-ing proven methods of philological and historical criticism to the biography of Muhammad. The way the two groups portray Muhammad teaches us more about the psychology of their epoch, the frameworks of their knowledge, and the presuppo-sitions of their culture than about the person of the Prophet himself.

Any biographic essay on Muhammad, or on any other religious figure, must begin by clarifying the relationship of mythical to historical knowledge in order to go be-yond both the mystical accounts presented within the Islamic tradition as historical facts and the withering criticism that strips religious consciousness of its living sub-stance. The first biography, written by Ibn Ishaq (d. 767) and known by the title of *Sīra,* mixes myth and history in an account that transformed the historical person and character of Muhammad. As a result, any study of Muhammad that is sensitive to the problems of historical psychology must incorporate the mythical *sīra* as it was understood in Ibn Ishaq's generation. Such a history would examine the rational and imaginary perception of the past; the relationship to the sacred, miracles, nature, and the supernatural; and the omnipresence of divine power, the creative power of speech, and communication with invisible beings such as angels, demons, God, and so forth.

Our culture can no longer move in this universe it calls magical, superstitious, un-real, irrational, imaginary, marvelous, fabulous, and legendary. All this vocabulary conveys difference, rejection, distance, and disqualification rather than integration into a comprehensive realm of intelligibility capable of accommodating all the facts and phenomena presented for analysis. The religious experience and historical activ-ity of Muhammad emerges and unfurls precisely in this semiological universe we no longer understand. To judge only from the irrefutable but too allusive testimony of the Qur'an and from accounts within the tradition, Muhammad's experience drew simultaneously on the collective memory of the ancient Near East,[2] represented in the great teachings and propagated by the peoples of the Book (*ahl al-kitāb*), and the living tradition of the Arab people, especially in the Hijaz region of Arabia.

For a period of at least twenty years there occurred an explosion of values, a kind of continuous creativity in which symbolic language constantly elevated and opened social and political behavior to the realm of transhistoric meanings. This was the role of Qur'anic discourse, which is always to be distinguished from the hadith, the written reports of what Muhammad and the Companions said or did.

People sometimes ask: "What did Muhammad *want?*" We have to ponder the pertinence of the question. Volition presupposes reflection, deliberation, strategy, and tactics aimed at reaching the targeted objective. Having assumed a position of responsibility for the community of believers, the Prophet had to think about means of protecting it so that the Message could reach the hearts of actual and potential believers and he could create the political and social conditions for a durable expansion of the new religion. But Muhammad exercised this volition in the psychological context of *wahy*—inspiration, eruption, revelation—all the while maintaining the place of the "I" in the communication space of Qur'anic discourse (*I/We—you—they/you*).

In that order of ideas, the question of whether Muhammad knew or did not know how to read and write (*al-nabiyy al-'ummī*) leads away from the psychological and cultural context of *wahy*. To know how to read and write requires, indeed, an exercise of reason quite apart from the improvisation, inventions, free associations, and flashes of thought to be found in prophetic discourse. Jack Goody has shown the great mental space opened up by "graphic reason" compared with oral reason.[3] It is from this perspective, the perspective of anthropological analysis of written and oral culture, that the biography (*Sīra*) of Muhammad must be reconsidered. The method of projecting all the great achievements of historical Islam backwards onto a reconstruction of Muhammad's life holds interest only insofar as the community needs to feed on mythologies. Of course it is true that not a single community anywhere, either religious or national, gets along without its mythologies.

What I have just said about Muhammad applies to all the founding prophets of religion. More generally, *mahdī* personalities, those of imams and of saints, still follow the founding model and demand the same approach. Through comparative studies of such phenomena we will succeed in enriching our knowledge of the "Human Experience of the Divine."[4]

Notes

1. The name of the Prophet has also been transcribed as Mohammed, Mohamed, and Mahomet in the West.—Trans.

2. See, for example, Sura 18.

3. See Jack Goody, *The Logic of Writing and the Organization of Society* (Cambridge: Cambridge University, 1986).

4. *L'expérience humaine du divin* is the title of a book by Michel Meslin (Paris: Editions du Cerf, 1988).

❧ 10 ❧

Hadith

Besides the Qur'an, what are the other fundamental texts of Islam?

The Qur'an is obviously the foremost foundational source of the Islamic religion. But apart from the Qur'an there exists a second source or foundation (*aṣl*): the prophetic tradition (*sunna*) known through the hadith, the Prophet's utterances in his role as guide of the Community of Believers and not as an instrument of divine will, transmitter of the Word of God.[1] Of course, since divine inspiration always drove the Prophet, what he said carried an ontological guarantee. Thus the Companions of the Prophet paid heed to his utterances, collected them with great piety, and transmitted them to subsequent generations. The Companions and subsequent followers constituted chains of witnesses (*isnād*) guaranteeing the authenticity of the reported utterances (*matn*). After the death of the Prophet these utterances became the object of an intense search so that they could be collected and put into writing as had been the Qur'an. Here, too, there occurred a transition from the oral tradition to the written.

The writing of the hadith took much more time than did the compilation of the Qur'an. The great collections of hadith deemed to be authentic were assembled only at the end of the ninth century, or long after the death of the Prophet. The selection and editing of these collections gave rise to ongoing controversies among the three great Muslim communities. Sunnis, for example, finally recognized the compilations of Bukhari (d. 870) and Muslim (d. 875), which they called the two authentic ones (*al-ṣaḥīḥayn*). The Twelver Shi'a staked their claim on the compilation entitled *Suitable for the Science of Religion,* started by Kulayni (d. 939) and supplemented by the collections of Ibn Babuyi (d. 991) and Tusi (d. 1067). The Khariji use the Ibn Habib collection (dating from the end of the eighth century) called *The True One of Spring* (*al-ṣaḥīḥ al-rabī*).

These manifest differences among the three traditional streams within Islam can be explained by the cultural origins of groups competing for control of the tradition, itself a conditioning factor for the legitimacy of caliphal authority, which was contested by the Shi'a and the Khariji. The ultimate object of the rivalry was leadership of the Muslim political community—caliphate or imamate, as the case might be; the rivalry was apparent in the very titles of the compilations taken as authority by each of the three streams of Islam, each of which considers the others to be contrived and false (*mukhtalaq*). Conscious of this situation, Muslim scholars known as the hadith folk, the *muḥaddithūn,* elaborated a critical science of hadith, an attempt at historical

45

verification of the chains of authority (*isnād*) and content (*matn*). But there has never been a general review of all the compilations—traditional and polemical positions aside—that would enable scholars to confront the essentially historical problem of exhaustively reconstructing the Islamic tradition. An attempt of this sort would presuppose a systematic comparison of all the *isnād* and all the texts carried forward in the three streams of the tradition so that the question of authenticity could be reexamined with modern means of investigation—including computers for the handling of texts—and of historical criticism.

Muslims have violently rejected suggestions of this sort already formulated by the Orientalist science of philology. The hadith, like the Qur'an, the *shari'a*, and pre-Islamic poetry, are a sensitive point in the Muslim consciousness. For that consciousness, the principles of criticism established even before the times of Bukhari, Muslim, Kulayni, and Tusi remain sufficient and definitive; the compilations put together on the basis of these principles constitute "official" and "closed" corpora, similar to the Qur'anic Corpus. The theological problem constituted by the simultaneous presence of three different closed official corpora, all regarded as official and complete, is either passed over in silence or overlooked according to the principle of orthodoxy defended by each tendency. Only a rigorous historical reassessment of the documentation, setting aside all preliminary conditions imposed by theology, can free up a state of affairs sanctified by more than ten centuries of scholastic repetition and community devotion.

The prophetic traditions (hadith) constitute a second foundation (*aṣl*) for the elaboration of the law. A critical treatment of the compilations would surely entail theoretical and practical consequences for the two legal sciences, *uṣūl* and *furū'*. And there we reach the heart of any modern critique of Islamic reason, an exhilarating task that requires epistemological commitment from Muslim researchers and freedom to think, write, publish, distribute, and teach from Muslim regimes.

A critique undertaken from the perspective of the exhaustive Islamic tradition would also open up the question of sects (*firaq*), of heresiography (*kutub al-milal wal-niḥal*), and hence of orthodoxy. I must say something of these things in order to assess the cultural, theological, and philosophical importance of a critique of Islamic reason.

According to a celebrated hadith, the Prophet announced that his community would be divided into seventy-three sects and that the members of all of these would go to hell except one, which was promised salvation. Sunnis use this hadith to show that they constitute a unique community called *ahl al-sunna wal-jamā'a,* those who follow the prophetic tradition and remain within the community. The Shi'a, on the other hand, teach that they alone managed to harvest the authentic heritage of the Qur'an and of the prophetic tradition, thanks primarily to the charisma and infallibility of the imams. They call themselves *ahl al-'iṣma wal-'adāla,* those who profess infallibility and justice. Finally, the Khariji lay claim to a greater chronological proximity to the founding moment (610–632), a guarantee of superior authenticity. They refused to recognize the Umayyads, whom they viewed as usurpers of the caliphate, and went out to fight—this is the sense of Khariji, which has been wrongly understood by Sunnis as secession from the community—in the name of a Qur'anic principle: that there is no authority except that of God, *lā ḥukma illā li-llāh*. They reject privilege of birth, such as descent from the Quraysh tribe or the Hashemite family of the Prophet, as a condition for acceding to the caliphate-imamate. They call themselves *al-shurāt,* those who sacrifice their lives to maintain the preeminent authority of God.

In all three cases we see the emergence of a religious consciousness bearing claims to rightfulness derived from Islamic teaching and the prophetic model. At the same time, this consciousness takes material form through political institutions and seeks fulfillment in them to direct the political community postulated by the Qur'an and the Prophet.

These self-evident tendencies find confirmation in declarations recorded rather tardily by historiographers, themselves actors inside the three ideological streams, each sublimating its historical meanderings in a spiritual epic. This sublimation of the history of Muslims in the seventh and eighth centuries continues to color the writing of history among current historians. Sublimation represents the psychological dimension of any history of "Islam," and a critique of Islamic reason must demonstrate its ideological impact.[2]

None of the three fractions posing as "orthodox" communities could base its "orthodoxy" solely on the only authority unanimously recognized by Muslims: the Qur'an. There is no authority but that of God! (*lā ḥukma illā li-llāh*). But we have also seen divergences in exegesis and how difficult it is to read the Qur'an in an unequivocal way that would lead to an orthodoxy binding on all believers and decisive on all debatable points. This impossibility of getting beyond a multiplicity of orthodoxies and rivalry among them can be explained by the ideological function of any religion. A religion serves social actors, who establish rival groups to assure their own control over symbolic goods without which political power cannot be assumed or exercised. Sociology and religious anthropology reveal what theological thought presents as religious "orthodoxy" to be the ideology of each group seeking to assert its supremacy. The ideological function of orthodoxy thus revealed has no name in theological discourse; we need a concept, therefore, that sums up the symbolic capital that is an "explicit" stake in the competition between political and economic forces, a stake that is concrete but hidden by "religious" vocabulary. Such analysis applies as much to the first century of Islam as to the current ventures of Islamist movements.

Notes

1. Western writers have frequently translated "hadith" as "tradition"; the term "prophetic tradition" used here reflects that practice and refers to the *sunna,* known through hadith. In the plural, the term "prophetic traditions" refers directly to the hadith. This use of the words "tradition" and "traditions" must not be confused with reference to the Islamic heritage as a whole,

the *turāth,* the "tradition." The *sunna* based in the hadith has helped shape the unfolding of that tradition.—TRANS.

2. My friend Hichem Djaït gave a series of lectures on the history of the seventh century at the Collège de France. Despite his familiarity with the exegeses of the "New History," he continued to bow before the constraints of what I call the spiritual epic of majoritarian Islam. See Djaït, *La grande discorde: religion et politique dans l'islam des origines* (Paris: Gallimard, 1989).

❧ 11 ❧

Tradition

What is tradition?

*W*e must come back to this concept, especially in view of what has just been said about the *sunna* and the hadith. For Muslims the prophetic tradition replaced, or at least ought to have replaced, all other forms of tradition and, in particular, the despotic customs of Arabia prevalent before the revelation to Muhammad and unrelated to the Divine Law. We once again encounter a conflict initiated by the Qur'an between science and knowledge (*'ilm*) uncovered and guaranteed by revelation, on the one hand, and the former traditions of all societies, such as that of pre-Islamic Arabia, called the *jāhiliyya,* the age of ignorance, on the other.

The scriptural tradition of the religions of the Book has given rise to the notion and historical practice subsumed under the term "societies of the Book/book." The constituted authorities in Christianity and Islam—minority status was more normal for Judaism before 1948—worked to substitute written law, either religious or secular, for the unwritten customs of local and provincial traditions. (Here once again anthropology needs to address these traditions, rejected and ignored as they have been by central religious and secular authority.) As a result, there are sedimentary levels of tradition where a certain ancient custom or belief can be found to have been integrated into and sanctified by the scriptural tradition. A sociological study of the application of the *shari'a* in contemporary Muslim societies would reveal three levels—not always hierarchical, often interacting with each other—in what has been broadly designated as the Islamic tradition:

1. The profound level, the cultural and customary pedestal of society, which emerges from ethnographic investigation and anthropological explanation.
2. The level of that which is "explicitly known" in the special language of what is called Muslim law but refers to that which is "implicitly lived" and therefore of great complexity for its fundamental links to the ethnographic level. The personal status of women, for example, illustrates a set of requirements issuing from a broad, implicitly lived domain, erased from and not recognized in the realm of that which is explicitly known. In a critical reevaluation of the law said to be Muslim, the study of this second level is another decisive chapter in the critique of Islamic reason.

49

3. The level of modern legal codes coexisting with the other two levels of prece-
dent in various circumstances and running from the case of Turkey to those of
the Sudan, Arabia, Pakistan, Algeria, and Tunisia. For example, the circumci-
sion of women continues to be practiced in parts of the Sudan and Egypt despite a proclaimed return to the *shari'a* and the introduction of modern legislation in many domains.

The issue of tradition follows naturally from the discussion of hadith. Since the
tradition recapitulates for the Community of Believers all propositions of truth, all
values, all norms of conduct revealed by God and taught by the Prophet, nothing can
be added from outside. Any practice or any new thought not sanctioned by the tradition must be rejected as innovation (*bid'a*). But the history and diversity of peoples
converted to Islam obviously required responses to many circumstances not foreseen
in either the Qur'an or the hadith. To be integrated into the tradition, these responses required sanction and sacralization either by reference to utterances of the
Prophet or by use of a method of reasoning called juridical *qiyās,* often translated as
"analogy." The method depends upon inference of legality from a base (*aṣl*), a similar
case from the founding period, that of the Prophet and the Pious Forefathers, *al-salaf
al-ṣāliḥ.*

In their struggle against innovations, the theologian-jurists aimed to protect "orthodox" dogmas and the integrity of the Islamic tradition against the ideas, customs,
and behaviors that actually constituted the "civilization of classical Islam" in the
period of the great caliphates (661–1258). We can distinguish two general attitudes toward the historical and sociological phenomenon of innovation. The rigorists, and
especially those recruited into the Hanbali school, are represented today by the Wahhabi ulema of Saudi Arabia. According to them, the tradition, the *sunna,* must prevail against all innovation. Moderates accept innovations that do not directly conflict
with an explicit text of law or a known teaching of the tradition.

This pair of ideas, tradition and innovation, must not only undergo analysis in
terms of theology and law but must also be treated more generally as an inherent dialectic in any society where several ethnocultural groups struggle either to augment
their dominance or to protect themselves from foreign elements. The Muslim political community found itself alternately in these two situations. In the period of the
conquests, the jurist-theologians tried to Islamicize the numerous contributions of
people converted to the new religion. They needed to maintain the preeminent position of religious law against ideological "identities" they considered dangerous innovations that would dissolve the very foundations of Islam. After the disappearance of
the caliphate and the rise of foreign powers in the East and West of the empire, the
Muslim political community, weakened and shrunk to a few urban centers, reinforced its means of defense by insisting on the notion of orthodoxy. The Wahhabi
movement in Arabia in the eighteenth century reactivated the dialectic between tradition and innovation in order to recreate a religious base for the political unification
of a society where segmentary structures had regained all their previous significance.

Likewise, during the period of colonial domination, the fight against innovations introduced by the West was a means of protecting the identity of Islam. With the Islamist movements begun by the Muslim Brothers in the 1930s in Egypt, vehement denunciation of Westernization took the dimensions of a political struggle. The genuinely religious stakes of the dialectic between tradition and innovation only appear as signals for rallying militants in that struggle.

As always we can find equivalent attitudes in the history of Judaism and Christianity. Locked into ghettos for centuries, Jews perpetuated their rabbinical tradition by rigorously controlling the intrusion of incompatible ideas and behaviors. Christians have fought against modernism and the forces of secularization since the sixteenth century. The psychocultural frameworks of that position are the same as those we have described for societies of the Book/book.

Framingham State College
Framingham, Massachusetts

⚜ 12 ⚜

The Ideal Community

How do the Qur'an and the tradition define the ideal human community?

Several issues turn out to be related to the notion of the ideal human community, including tolerance, the perception of non-Muslims, and the status of protected groups (*dhimmī*) such as Jews and Christians, especially in the caliphal period. And I cannot sidestep a problem that is current in the West, in the Muslim world, and indeed in all contemporary societies: human rights.

The great importance and, on occasion, tragic urgency of the issues grouped together here make them suitable material for a great book. I dream of a book that would reconsider the pathetic cry of Abu Hayyan al-Tawhidi in the tenth century, "Man is a problem for man," in the light of the whole cultural, political, and social history of "Islam."

In which field of intelligibility must we seek pertinent responses to serious questions about the ideal human community, religious freedom, and the rights of man? An attentive reader will already have discerned my constant uneasiness about the theoretical conditions of knowledge—that is, about the epistemological standing of discourse—usually invoked in the treatment of a great religious tradition. The Islamic tradition, like the Christian or Jewish tradition, assumes a privileged position of doctrinal authority over every issue that arises in history; only the tradition holds the "correct" principles and methodology for bringing forth responses consistent with the set of values, beliefs, and models of action needed to keep the faithful on the narrow path leading to salvation in this life and beyond. In laying claim to a monopoly on "correct" methodology, the tradition proclaims with one stroke its dominance over all scientific disciplines, which must collaborate in the exercise of its control. The claim gives birth to irremediable tension between the scholars who exercise doctrinal authority and the specialists in relevant disciplines, such as history, sociology, psychology, linguistics, and semiology.

To get beyond this tension, I will continue to incorporate the techniques of argument and the contents of tradition in a general analysis where rights to critical epistemology prevail both for the Pious Ancestors and for us today. These rights must be put at the same level of transcendence with regard to ideological commitments, and by that I mean independence, as are the "rights of God" (*ḥuqūq allah*), which are so perfectly defined and scrupulously respected in the Sufi itinerary.

Let's start then from the answers of the Qur'an and the tradition. The ideal human community is the *umma muhammadiyya,* the group of disciples, initially small, weak, and threatened, that grew larger thanks to the direct help of God and the action of the Prophet, who was consistently enlightened by *wahy.* After the death of the Prophet, the vicars (caliphs and/or imams) piously and rigorously protected the spiritual heritage, broadened the diffusion of Islam, and consolidated for earthly history the *umma*'s calling as repository, witness, and actor of the final revelation, made to the Seal of the Prophets (*khatam al-anbiya*).

I have shown how this *umma* took its place in the universe of communication appropriate to Qur'anic discourse; the "they" at first designated the opponents of Muhammad but was subsequently stretched theologically to include all non-Muslims, who were already differentiated at the Qur'anic stage between a "you," believers and nonbelievers, and a "they," applied to atheists and the recalcitrant. Such are the ideal community's sociological origins in Arabia, historical development in the Muslim political community turned empire, and theological roots in Qur'anic discourse and its legal-theological extension.

The members of this *umma* are reputed to have replicated in ideal fashion all the constitutive habits of Qur'anic anthropology. In Qur'anic discourse, the human being (*insān*)—or the people, the descendants of Adam, humankind (*al-nās, banū ādam, al-bashar*)—is constantly questioned. More than angels, jinn, or Satan, human beings are the permanent objects of God's attention. The relationship is lived, experiential, traceable to Qur'anic discourse, transmissible, and reproducible by this same discourse in each individual experience. Within this relationship the ideal member of the *umma* takes shape psychologically, spiritually, and corporally (through ritual practices). For that person, the heart is the profound "I," the home of all the energies of the spirit (*rūh*), of the soul (*nafs*), and of the body. The Word of God resounds in the heart, and the spiritual instinct is stimulated there, insofar as other instincts are disciplined enough and trained enough to extract from the verses all the significations, the sign-symbols linking the cosmos, the external world, and profane history with God, bridging the abyss between the act of creation (by fiat, or *kun*) and the objective world so created.

The notion of ideal community postulated and made possible by models and definitions of Qur'anic anthropology reminds one at critical points of that proposed by the founders of the Eastern church.[1] This community draws its energy, its cohesion, its persistence through history and its capacity to live in the present world partially and sporadically (thanks to the contemplative orders and the Sufi way) from mythical reference to an inaugural moment and event that separate time and space between sacred and profane, before and after. The mythical vision is completed by postulating an ideal transmission of all these events, words, and models known by a privileged generation, the contemporaries of the inaugural age: disciples and companions who would narrate all that they had seen and heard and would thus condition the perennial nature and spiritual quality of the ideal community. Another postulate, also mythical in essence, is the intellectual capacity attributed to the learned men who had the "scientific" responsibility of extracting all meanings of the Word of God and enunciating them in the incisive, unambiguous forms of juridical discourse.

The ideal *umma* cannot have historical existence without these postulates for constructing a mythical consciousness, which depends upon a portrayal of the inaugural age for its effectiveness and translation into history. That is why all current Islamic discourse tries hard to compel respect for the "historical" validity of the model handed down by the inaugural age. Islamist militants refuse to recognize that myth plays a specific role in energizing the consciousness of actors but cannot be confused with the concrete historical products of that consciousness. As a result, the Islamists move further away from both the inaugural age from which they seek inspiration and the concrete factors shaping historical action.

I am now prepared to consider the problems of tolerance, of the status of non-Muslims, and of human rights without introducing anachronisms, which are all too common in analyses of this sort. In the implacable struggle pitting Arabs against Israelis, Westerners often project accusations of intolerance, violence, and violation of human rights backwards on the period of classical Islam. All these notions depend upon modern, recent, and yet uncertain definitions. Moreover, polemicists of every origin and religious persuasion deliberately ignore the historical reality I am trying so obstinately to establish here. Mythical structures, semiological bases, hermeneutical conditions, spiritual disciplines, mimetic overbidding—these factors created and energized the consciousness of the ideal community, on the one hand, and produced the history of the societies of the Book/book, on the other. They are common to Jews, Christians, and Muslims. A critique leveled at any one of these traditions, whether anachronistic or pertinent, necessarily hits the other two as well. (On at least certain points, however, such as slavery and the status of foreigners, I set aside the case of Judaism, insofar as it has been sociologically minoritarian and lacking in state support.)

The concept of tolerance is a modern achievement that cannot be dissociated from the philosophical critique of truth. Muslims, like Christians, started from a claim to revealed truth as a basis for legislation, a revealed truth that was unique, absolute, unchangeable, beyond historicity, understood and correctly carried forward by those and those alone who declared their faith in all the dogmas constituting this truth. Jews and Christians refused to recognize the prime dogma of Islam: the Qur'an as the Word of God, revealed to human beings through the mediation of Muhammad, His Messenger. Jews did the same thing with respect to Christians, who did it with regard to Jews and Muslims. Within this definition of truth, one can only build theologies and sociopolitical orders functioning as *mutually exclusive cultural and legal systems*. The reciprocity of exclusions is complete and without exception. A reciprocity of consciousness as a base for an exchange of rights and duties on a level of legal equality would come only after there occurred an epistemological, hence mental, break with the concept of theological truth developed in the three revealed religions.

There are obviously instances where implementation of the legal-theological orders defined by each of the religions has been more or less humane and open to nonnegligible forms of tolerance and other instances, to the contrary, of violent, inquisitorial implementation. On the tolerance scale Islam surely does not rank last. Without falling into the sort of self-indulgence that seeks to absolve Islam of practices and conceptions characteristic of certain periods of history, Westerners must follow the lead of historians in recognizing that Muslim ethics demonstrated a concern both for rendering the fate of slaves more tolerable and for respecting the religious dignity of "people of the Book" (*ahl al-kitāb*) above and beyond legal regulations. Although they recognized freedom of religion, however, these regulations also stressed the social and political inferiority of unmistakable rivals to "true religion" (*dīn al-ḥaqq* in the Qur'an), which, transformed into historic Islam, was obliged to cohabit with peoples of the Book. Jews and Christians, even when reduced to the status of *dhimmī,* never ceased to proclaim in a copious and polemical literature their callings as ideal communities enjoying the promise of salvation. We must interpret all the relationships of domination and, now and then, communication among the three monotheistic families in this context of mimetic rivalry to incarnate, live, and defend "true religion." The idea of tolerance would emerge slowly, with great difficulty, and in ever precarious fashion through the excesses of the inquisition, persecution, and wars of religion, as they are called in the West.

What I have just said about tolerance applies to the whole set of human rights. Revelation as collected in the sacred writings contains starting points, strong roots, and carrier concepts for the emergence of the person as a subject equipped with rights and as an agent responsible for the observance of obligations toward God and peers in the political community. The idea of peers does not coincide, of course, with the modern idea of citizens, abstracted as it is from religious beliefs and philosophical positions. I have just shown that the person postulated by revelation is the believer who adheres to a set of dogmas and who translates this adherence into strict observance of the "rights of God." The rights of "peers" thus defined comes to be incorporated as duty insofar as each believer respects the rights of God in the first place. The rights/duties pair reacquires in effectiveness and spiritual content that which is lost by extension sociologically: The nonbeliever must be reduced to an inferior status and even fought.

Sura 9 of the Qur'an illustrates very clearly the theological and sociopolitical framework for applying the rights/duties pair to human beings in society (believers among themselves, believers and nonbelievers, believers and *ahl al-kitāb*), although these rights and duties take their full value and full scope only if there is, first of all, respect for the rights of God. Sura 9 is chronologically one of the last. Muhammad and his followers had just returned victoriously to Mecca. The Muslims could now reinvest with new religious expression all the symbolism of that ancient Arab religion attached to the *ka'ba,* which became the House of God. The danger of a victory of polytheists over believers was already removed, and it was possible to set down the rights and duties of the groups in question: the believers who formed the core of the new *umma,* the *ahl al-kitāb,* and the polytheists, principally bedouins (*a'rāb*), who had refused to join the Prophet in battle (jihad) when he was exposed to threat. Here are the verses:

> After the sacred months have run out, kill the polytheists wherever you find them; capture them, besiege them, ambush them. (Verse 5)
> When they defeat you, they do not respect either alliance or pact that would assure you protection. They seek to please you with their words, but they are rebels at heart: the majority of them are perverse. (Verse 8)
> Those who have believed, those who have emigrated, those who have fought in the path of God with their goods and their person will be placed in a very high row near God: There are the victors. (Verse 20)
> Oh you who believe! Don't take your fathers and brothers as friends, if they prefer unbelief to faith; those of you who would take them as friends would be unjust. (Verse 23)
> Ask for pardon for them or do not ask pardon for them; if you ask for pardon for them seventy times, God will not pardon them, because they are absolutely unbelieving toward God and his Prophet. God does not guide perverse people. (Verse 80)
> When God takes you toward a group of these people and they ask your permission to go off on a campaign, tell them: "You will not ever go with me; you will not ever fight an enemy with me. You have been happy to stay home on the first occasion; remain then with those who stay in the rear." (Verse 83)
> But there is a reason to get angry with those who ask you to spare them from combat, because they are rich and because they would be happy to remain with those who stay in the rear. (Verse 93)

One should read the whole sura. It raises extremely delicate problems by sharply defining the legal-theological status of social categories in a style that is direct, concrete, and occasionally almost judicial or military. One is thus tempted to take all these declarations literally and to come away with a negative image of Islam, which rendered this set of verses into legal code. But such an interpretation would be totally anachronistic, since it would project backwards the current philosophy of human rights and would ignore the fundamental lesson of the sura as a whole, which is *not outmoded.* Muslim theological thought has not committed itself to the kind of modern interpretation that would highlight the pivotal problem still lurking in the contemporary discourse on human rights.

One can gauge the extent and frequency of that problem by reading contributions to the volume published by UNESCO entitled *Philosophical Foundations of Human Rights.*[2] All the authors, who are of diverse national origin and ideology, recognize that successive declarations of human rights since 1789 have been without effect for millions of persons because they have not been accompanied by sanctions. There has been no high court, independent of all constituent states and capable of violating the taboos and definitions of all local cultures, to pronounce and apply sanctions. But the constitution of such a court would encounter the difficulty not yet surmounted, and perhaps insurmountable, that is enunciated clearly in the whole of Sura 9.

The Qur'an declares without ambiguity the "criteria" that guarantee for eternity not just human rights but also human salvation. This is the point of verses 20, 71–72, and 112, to which one must add all those verses that address believers directly in their privileged relationship of *I/We—You*. The criteria embedded in Sura 9 are more explicit, for it contrasts the positive conditions fulfilled by believers with the negative attitudes of opponents, who have no rights: They must be fought and ejected from the Community because they refused to commit themselves to it spontaneously at the moment when believers were not yet dominant.

What is interesting about Sura 9 is that a discourse of human rights emerges in the course of social confrontations among poor, defenseless, subordinate social groups who agree to go fight,[3] the rich who find excuses to be relieved of such duties, and the bedouins who do not give up their false beliefs. The proclamation of human rights in France in 1789 came out of similar circumstances. Both cases concern at once universal, abstract human beings and concrete, socially and ideologically defined human beings in the midst of an irremediably divided society: believers and nonbelievers in the Qur'an; rising bourgeoisie and privileged classes (nobility and clergy) in the French Revolution.

In the Qur'an, the contingent conditions prevailing in Arabia (poverty, sociopolitical hierarchy based on birth, social disintegration, and deflation of what was formerly sacred) are transcended by the introduction of "absolute" criteria: the cause of God, who is one, living, just, vigilant, helping, forgiving, all powerful, and welcoming to all those who would open their hearts and enter into the Covenant. Wars waged for human cause can be regarded as genuine, valid, and sacred only if undertaken within the perspective of the cause of God.

The discourse of transcendence and of absoluteness opens an infinite space for the promotion of the individual beyond the constraints of fathers and brothers, clans and tribes, riches and tributes; the individual becomes an autonomous and free person, enjoying a liberty guaranteed by obedience and love lived within the alliance. The consciousness of the person thus liberated does not even require the mediation of another human consciousness, as it does in Christianity, which depends on the mediation of Jesus; the ontological access of a Muslim is direct, total, and irreversible. The contextual decision of the Muslim judge is external to his consciousness. That decision puts his consciousness back into direct contact with the *ḥukm allah*, divine jurisdiction. The judge is but an enunciator, and the caliph or imam only a guarantor of its application.

Qur'anic discourse has broadly demonstrated its efficacy as a space for the emergence, training, and deployment of the free person, who enjoys guarantees of life, property, family, and private domicile not as a "citizen" of a civil society managed by elected representatives or by universal suffrage (sovereign of the nation founded in 1789 by the French Revolution) but as God's partner in an eternal compact.

What has happened to the English and French revolutions? The French celebrated the bicentennial of the French Revolution in 1989. It was interesting to observe every ceremony, speech, initiative, and appeal and to identify the modes of perception and the relationships established between the inaugural event, the historical antecedents that engendered it, and the ways it has been applied in France, Europe, and the rest of the world. In the cultural, intellectual, and historical climate of today, there is a vital and urgent need to reflect upon the symbols at stake in the passage from a doctrine of human rights linked to the respect of each conscience for the rights of God toward a new doctrine of human rights left to the appreciation of other human beings, those brought to power by the exercise of popular sovereignty. As historians, sociologists, and anthropologists, we can draw comparative pictures of the two systems, which followed each other in time and which coexist in an impenetrable way within the secret consciences of those who still believe but have been destined to meet in an unequal confrontation, ever since the great rupture of 1789, between the unfinished structure of democracy and spiritual authority. Such authority has not succeeded in restoring revelation to its role of disclosure, advent, and creation of space for the realization of the person, where dogmatic partition between believers and nonbelievers would be abolished in favor of the principles of liberty, equality, and fraternity—the principles that express the revolutionary essence of the Revolution.

What revealed religions can say to the revolutionary phenomenon that rejected their symbolism in order to end social and political inequalities is that every revolution takes root in a concrete historical context that limits the transcendental or transhistoric scope of revolutionary intent. The positions assumed by the Prophet in his fight against opponents who sought to liquidate him were inevitable; so were most of the death sentences handed down by the French revolutionaries. In both cases, a human price was paid for the *survival* of a progressive vision of the human condition. Religions, like the great secular revolutions, must recognize and overcome a common difficulty: that the positive view of personhood is regularly confiscated by ecclesiastical and state institutions, which aim to reestablish hierarchies and inequalities or let new ones spring up, whether in religious societies such as the Islamic Republic of Iran or in liberal Western democracies, not to mention those crushing failures, the democracies that called themselves "popular."

The decidedly perilous parallelism that I am trying to sketch between the spiritual ethos of great revolutions and that of revelation would be deemed unacceptable by theologians from both ends of the spectrum: managers of the sacred establishment, on the one hand, and preachers of lay militancy, on the other. Indeed, both groups would wish to revive all the old concepts they and others have manipulated but never tried to reconcile within a single field of intelligibility. Such a field, as a matter of fact, would result from a general reevaluation of the whole historical path leading from revelation (to include salvation history considered beyond the confines of dogmatic closure) to secular revolutions, beginning with the English, American, and French.

We may reformulate the question about the ideal human community in a more provocative way: What are the philosophical criteria that secular revolution has substituted for those of revelation to promote the triumph of the new political, social, and symbolic order? The question presupposes the following points:

1. Revelation committed the person to an experience of the divine where the respect of rights was guaranteed by the internalization of ontological primacy and the ethical priority of the rights of God as they are enunciated in revealed discourse.

2. Theological discourse transforms revealed discourse into dogmatic closure whereby only "orthodox" believers enjoy in full the rights recognized by revelation. In this way the social hierarchies and political, economic, and cultural inequalities revelation sought to abolish are reconstituted. The theological and juridical reading of Sura 9 engenders dogmatic closure, while the reattachment of that sura to the general sweep of Qur'anic discourse would maintain an opening toward the spiritual vocation of the person.

3. Secular revolution[4] breaks up hierarchies and intolerable inequalities created with the help of sacralizing power exercised by the agents controlling dogmatic closure, who claim to act as the authorized interpreters of revelation. Revolution thus reveals a hidden function of the sacred conveyed by religions: the constant passage from transcendence, which opens up an infinitude of meaning, to transcendentalization, which fixes meaning within doctrinal systems, political orders, and legal codes. It is intellectual and scientific modernity, inseparable from an open-ended secularism, that permits this disclosure of hidden stakes in all the discursive practices of human beings in society.

4. The example of the French Revolution of 1789–1792 shows how the discursive activity of social actors can reintroduce sacralizing and transcendentalizing functions into a context "liberated" from traditional religions. Republican France has been resacralized thanks to the (re)construction of a national, secular imaginary. The nationalisms of the nineteenth century and their expansion beyond Europe in the twentieth have carried with them the double process of breaking with the former religious realm of sacredness (desacralization and detranscendentalization) and installing a "secular," republican realm of sacredness with the imaginary to go with it.[5]

Notes

1. See Thomas Spidlik, *La spiritualité de l'Orient chrétien* (Rome: Orientalia Cristiana, 1978).

2. UNESCO, A. Diemer et al., *Philosophical Foundations of Human Rights* (Lanham, Md.: UNIPUB, 1986).

3. See Verse 60 on alms for the poor and needy; Verse 117 on the Emigrants and the Helpers who followed the Prophet.

4. I am thinking of 1789 in France, 1917 in Russia, 1952 in Egypt, and so on; we need a typology of revolutions according to their capacity to symbolize human existence.

5. See *Archives des sciences sociales des religions* 66, 1 (1988); the issue is devoted to revolution and religions.

❧ 13 ❧

Women

What is the status of women according to the Qur'an and according to the wider tradition as interpreted by various "orthodoxies"?

*T*his question arises inevitably when one approaches the subject of Islam for a Western audience. Muslims themselves come back more and more to this issue, which feeds sharp polemics and, more rarely, fresh insights, especially about the contribution of the Qur'an.

People repeat so many devastating banalities about the status of women in "Islam" that I would like to shift the analysis and questions toward heretofore neglected domains. I will be careful not to spirit away the true issues by reasserting that the Qur'an improved the status of women, raising them to the same spiritual dignity as men, or that women in "Islam" are not subjected, as are their sisters in the West, to fierce social and economic competition with men. Muslims militating for an Islamic model of human rights often advance such arguments. Westerners, inversely, emphasize the intolerable inferiority of women in Muslim societies, citing polygamy, divorce by repudiation, the wearing of the veil, segregation of the sexes, imprisonment in household tasks, strict dependence on the husband, and lack of legal rights. Those who have generated these images, positive or negative, have neglected to begin by considering the givens of the feminine condition common to all societies, givens that persist in our time despite numerous efforts at emancipation, especially in the modern West.

When the Qur'an appeared in history, it could not modify two essential aspects of entrenched and centuries-old conditions: elementary kinship structures and control of sexuality. On other important matters such as inheritance, integrity of the body, and access to social, cultural, and political advantages, customs quite foreign to the prescriptions of the Qur'an and the norms of Muslim law continued to prevail among many social groups. For that reason we need to examine the situation not only for each society but for every ethnocultural group that until recently stayed outside the domain where Muslim law was applied. The Kabylia region of Algeria, where Muslim law began to be applied only in 1962, would be an example.

Claude Lévi-Strauss long ago showed the role elementary kinship structures play in the circulation of wealth and power among persons in a society. Patterns in the exchange of women follow from strategies of enrichment, domination, and auto-protection that take precedence over the interests of the persons exchanged. The security of the individual is linked to the power of the clan assuring his or her protection; while the man never leaves the family, the woman may pass into another class to cement an alliance. That is why the control of female sexuality is rigorously defined in the code of honor that continues to prevail in many Mediterranean societies of both Christian and Muslim traditions. Even in Yemen and Arabia, cradle of Islam, bedouin rights have not been entirely replaced by Muslim law.[1] Authors such as Joseph Schact[2] have evoked links between Muslim law and local "substrata," but the most pertinent question about the status of women is the extent to which the new provisions introduced by the Qur'an modified the operation of elementary lineage structures rather than just certain legal provisions and the ethical-religious framework of former systems. The persistence even today of different socialization practices for daughter and son reflects the mother's internalization of an objectively unfavorable status reproduced through daughters to assure the survival of a system above and beyond the moral and religious calling of the person recognized by the Qur'an. This fact tends to prove that Qur'anic legislation acts on the dignity of the person more than on structures. Only a precise sociological study of the application of Muslim law in each society could permit a refinement of the distinction I am suggesting between the weight, permanence, and preeminence of structures, on the one hand, and the Qur'an's modification of the ethical-religious framework for the system governing the exchange of persons and wealth, on the other.

The biological makeup of women engages them in the reproduction of life and hence in the distribution of the most precious good in any society. Everywhere women have been the "object" of strategies on the part of men, who have a monopoly of control over the distribution of goods and power relationships among families, clans, and tribes. It was only with the appearance of biological means of liberation such as the contraceptive pill that the emancipation of the feminine condition could reach down to the level of strategies as old as human societies. But then there emerged that vast continent of sexuality and all the taboos to repress it, regulated by an implacable moral code, which was said to be "ethical" and "religious." The historical, cultural, political, economic, and democratic circumstances in which these debates began to be heard in Muslim societies invite us to exercise great prudence, patience, and indulgence before pronouncing peremptory condemnations in the manner of legitimately indignant "feminists" or, in contrast, making self-confirming speeches to defend the status of women as being of divine origin, intangible, and superior to all that human beings have otherwise imagined.

In light of the perspectives opened up by this problematic, it becomes clear that it would be premature and derisory to engage in debate about the Qur'anic verses that speak of polygamy, repudiation, inheritance, the "superiority" of men over women, the veil, lineage, and licit and illicit marriage. All these verses have already been the object of juridical explication carried on by the great jurists—the exegetes and founders of schools of interpretation (those whom the tradition calls *al-a'imma al-mujtahidūn,* such as Al-Shafi'i and Ja'far al-Sadiq). In this way we find ourselves up against a body of law that judges apply wherever central authority has managed to establish Muslim judicial organization (although there are sectors in which that organization never existed or where it worked in parallel with former customs).

There is one important, essentially psychological factor that shapes behavior today even among Muslims who have long been established in Western societies: It involves what I have called the *sacralization* and *transcendentalization* of norms, whether ethical or juridical or of Qur'anic or archaic origin. These are the first two levels of the tradition as they were defined in Chapter II. The cultural framework for the socialization of children (with major differences between girls and boys) is still deeply colored by the religious vision inspired by collective celebrations, festivals, individual and collective rituals, and various *signals* of "Islamic" identity. This vision has become the central theme of the ideologies of political struggle. The processes of sacralization and transcendentalization have become more active and *ambiguous* by virtue of the fact that political claims have relegated theological reflection to disuse and oblivion. Yet in classical Islamic political thought it was such reflection that sustained interest in preserving the sacred and transcendent realm of the Qur'an from contamination, deviancies, and perversions due to what were called sects and heresies. We may thus articulate a tendency in the current process of socialization: The more the traditional realm of the sacred is ideologized for political ends, the greater the disfunctionalities in the status of women on the ethnographic and Islamic levels of the tradition and the more passage to a kind of ill-dominated modernity works itself out in personal dramas (suicides, depression, rejections, alienation) and great social upheavals (violence, demonstrations, revolution).

I cannot close this analysis and these appeals for a cultural revolution that would for the first time integrate the emancipation of women into a modern philosophy (yet to be written) of the human being without paying homage to generations of women who have assured the survival of our species at the expense of their self-realization as *persons,* inviolable loci of creative liberty. Women have insured this survival through the function of reproduction, gestation, and primary socialization of the child; to do that they have *incorporated* in the physical sense not only the germs of life but, to their own detriment, the "ethical," "religious," and "juridical" norms that consecrate their status as "object" and "symbol" in the strategies of exchange, domination, and self-defense.

How many women, either in the Third World or in Western societies, have mastered the biological, anthropological, historical, and sociocultural genesis of the condition of women in order to lead the battle for emancipation at the appropriate levels and in the interest of promoting the human being? I offer these ideas as a man who learned and retained a great deal from his illiterate mother. She was perfectly integrated into a society marked by the effects of long-term interaction between the first and second levels of the tradition (see Chapter II) but brutally thrown into dramas of uprootedness during the last thirty years, since Algerian independence.[3]

The reader will have to pardon me for not having undertaken a detailed analysis of numerous verses that for centuries fixed the status of women. Such work has not yet been done in the context of a critique of Islamic reason. In addition, the restricted format of this book, which rather aims to open up new fields for research, knowledge, and reflection in the Islamic domain, does not permit inclusion of such a discussion.[4]

Notes

1. See J. Chelhod, *Le droit bédouin* (Paris: Petite bibliothèque sociologique internationale, 1971).

2. See Joseph Schact, *An Introduction to Islamic Law* (Oxford: Clarendon, 1964).

3. See Fatima Mernissi, *Beyond the Veil: Male-Female Dynamics in Modern Muslim Society,* rev. ed. (Bloomington, Ind.: Indiana University Press, 1987).

4. For a concrete example of the theoretical difficulties raised *today* by recourse to the Qur'an, see my study of Verse 12 of Sura 4, "De *Ijtihäd* à la critique de la raison islamique: lecture du verset IV, 12," *Lectures du Coran,* 2nd rev. ed. (Tunis: Alif, 1991).

❧ 14 ❧

Dogmas

Are there dogmas in Islam? If so, what are they?

Every religion embraces beliefs and nonbeliefs that have been passed on as untouchable, indisputable truths. That is to say, there are dogmas that elude any critical questioning by the faculty of reason and establish the contents of the faith. In Islam, for example, five dogmas specify ritual obligations: the profession of faith, or *shahāda*; prayer; the giving of alms according to legal standards; the fast of Ramadan; and the pilgrimage to Mecca.

Dogmas are defined by the Qur'an and then elaborated and reinvoked by "orthodox" authorities each time it is necessary to refute opinions deemed to be heterodox. That is why there exists a catechistic literature (*'aqīda*) that synthesizes Qur'anic pronouncements into concise propositions.[1] Sura 112 defines the basic dogma of the Islamic faith: "Recite: it is He, God, One, the impenetrable Absolute. He does not procreate; He is not procreated; nothing is equal to him."

All other dogmas flow from the attestation of God, one, absolute, transcendent and from his decision to choose Muhammad as His Messenger to reveal the Qur'an. That is the object of the *shahāda,* which includes two parts: "There is no divinity other than Allah; and Muhammad is the Messenger of Allah." Jews and Christians accept the first proposition but reject the second. "Allah" is the proper name God takes for himself in Arabic.

It would take too long to enumerate all the articles in the profession defining the faith of a Muslim. The last judgment, the resurrection of the body, eternal recompense, paradise and hell, angels, jinn, prophets—all are points that require the validation of the faith, *imān.*

The acceptance of dogmas must be translated into good works (*a'māl*): compliance with prescribed rituals and application of the regulations (*ahkām*) defined by the law, *al-shari'a.* The link to dogmas reinforces the previously mentioned sacralization of law and of all conduct to which it is applied.[2]

For certain schools of theology such as the Mu'tazili, dogmas became the object of rational speculation in the interest of discovering a measure of coherence acceptable at least to the elites (*al-khāṣṣa*). A famous example is the theory of the created Qur'an, which the caliphs Al-Ma'mum (813–833), Al-Mu'tasim (833–842), and Al-Wathiq (842–847) decided to prescribe as official dogma, thereby arousing the opposition of Ibn Hanbal (d. 855). The caliph Al-Qa'im (d. 1031) later ordered the famous profession of faith called *al-qādiriyya* to be read in the mosques of Baghdad, forbidding specifically any reference to the dogma of the created Qur'an.

This example shows how dogmas become stakes in the game of politics. In the history of Christianity, equivalent examples include the Nicene Creed (325) and the Chalcedon Creed (451), which led to the creation of the Coptic Monophysite church, the symbol of Athanasius (before 670). As in Islam and Judaism, obedience to the law is obligatory for all faithful Christians who declare their faith in dogmas. Pope John Paul II restored this link by insisting on respect for the fundamental teachings of the Catholic church despite increasing resistance from secular morality, and societies that regarded themselves as definitively liberated are witnessing a return to religion.

Contrary to the constraining dogmas of revealed religions, the Buddha preached liberty from all dogmatic teaching:

> Yes, Kālāmas, it is proper that you have doubt, that you have perplexity, for a doubt has arisen in matter which is doubtful. Now, look you Kālāmas, do not be led by reports, or tradition, or hearsay. Be not led by the authority of religious texts, nor by mere logic or inference, nor by considering appearances, nor by the delight in speculative opinions, nor by seeming possibilities, nor by the idea: "this is our teacher." But, O Kālāmas, when you know for yourselves that certain things are unwholesome (akusala), and wrong, and bad, then give them up. ... And when you know for yourselves that certain things are wholesome (kusala) and good, then accept them and follow them.[3]

This stance against dogma contrasts with the violent clashes over dogmas among peoples of the Book and within Christianity and Islam. Such comparisons between religions of the Book and traditions heretofore largely ignored in the West show why the West must be defined to include Islam.

Notes

1. For a good example, see *La profession de foi d'Ibn Batta,* translated by Henri Laoust (Damascus: Institut français, 1958).

2. Ignac Goldziher has illustrated this link between Islamic dogma and Islamic law very well. See his *Introduction to Islamic Theology and Law* (Princeton: Princeton University, 1981).

3. Walpola Rahula, *What the Buddha Taught* (New York: Grove, 1974), pp. 2–3.

❧ 15 ❧

Sacerdotal Power

Is there a sacerdotal role in Islam? How do the faithful enter into a relationship with the divine?

*P*osed in this way, the question is more useful than one often asked about the absence of a clergy in Islam. The sacerdotal function is, in effect, more general and more fundamental than that assigned to a clergy; it is to be found in various forms and with various formalities in all monotheistic and polytheistic religions. Thus we are talking about a function of anthropological significance.

Among the ancient Jews, sacerdotal power lay in offering victims to God; among the Romans, in a polytheistic context, those who carried out sacrifices to the gods were responsible for gaining their protection. In all cases the central action, laden with meaning, was the sacrifice (*al-ḍahiyya*). The sacrifice itself served to put the faithful in contact with the divine; those who had the power to effect sacrifice were thus the mediators guaranteeing the validity of the sacrifice and its propitiating, conciliating, or redeeming efficacy.

Priests perform the sacerdotal function as an act of mediation in Christianity. The priest is one who is qualified to appear in the face of God and to address him without intermediary. Reduced to symbolic procedures, the sacrifice comes as a part of the mass (Eucharist). There is no sacerdotal power in this sense in Islam; each believer enters into a direct relationship with God in prayer, makes the pilgrimage to Mecca (*ḥajj*), individually fulfills the duties of fasting during Ramadan, and performs almsgiving as specified by the law. Each year, during the pilgrimage to Mecca, each Muslim must sacrifice an animal, which is usually a sheep. Here then Muslims rediscover the notion of mediation, of propitiatory action, of search for contact with the divine, but there is no such task assigned to priests as there is in Christianity. The imam who leads the ranks of the faithful in collective prayer has no sacerdotal function. He distinguishes himself from the rest of the faithful by occupying a niche in the mosque called the *miḥrāb* to symbolize the unity of the community at prayer.

In what is called popular religion, the cult of saints has conferred upon certain religious personalities, called marabouts or *walī*, friends of God, a status that resembles the sacerdotal function of priests. Saints have the power of intercession before God; they address him directly so that the wishes of the faithful may be heard. The faithful make frequent pilgrimages to benefit from the blessings (*baraka*) of living saints or to invoke the compassion of dead saints by staying near their tombs. "Orthodox" Islam obviously condemns such beliefs and practices, which have nonetheless always prevailed, even in the cities.

There is not in Islam a hierarchical organization possessing spiritual powers, much less political power, of the type held by the Catholic church before the separation of church and state in the West. There does exist a corps of experts in the law, theologian-jurists who supervise orthodoxy and the application of religious law in conjunction with the state. In classical Islam and in contemporary regimes, the learned men (ulema) have played a role similar in many respects to that held by clerks in the Catholic church before separation. The *mufti,* the qadi, the jurist, the imam, and the theologian together constitute a corps of personnel (ulema) that is both religious and lay. Theoretically the great legal experts can affirm their independence vis-à-vis the state, but the state today has tighter supervision over this personnel than in the classical era. In exchange, the ulema help legitimate established authority and protect the state against assault by religious extremists.

﷽ 16 ﷽

Authority

How are the domains of spiritual and political authority delineated in Islam?

This question approaches one of the most fundamental, most searing, most debated, and, as a result, most embroiled issues in Islamic thought. The great quarrel that erupted in 661 and led to the breakup of the *umma* concerned relationships of hierarchy between authority and power.

Historically it is difficult to recapture the vocabulary used by actors in the drama that began with the death of the Prophet in 632. Most accounts employ vocabulary from a later period, which tends to portray an essentially political and social contest for control of the new state created by the Prophet in Medina as theological. Clan struggle, so characteristic of segmentary societies like that of Arabia, had not of course been suppressed by the new religion; thus the Hashemite clan of the Quraysh tribe, the tribe to which the Prophet belonged, pursued its long-term rivalry with the Banu Sufyan. Muhammad's political and religious success constituted a new factor and simply served to complicate this rivalry.

The Qur'an and the teaching of Muhammad indisputably opened up new political horizons, which were extended and transcendentalized by the eschatological perspective and the sense of God's absoluteness. That is what I call the founding experience of Medina, for it was in Medina that religious preaching assumed its first political incarnations. Muhammad brought together the charisma of the Messenger of God, transmitter of revelation; the authority of the chief, who decides disputes and guides the community of the faithful; and the power of decision in matters of conflict between "believers" and "infidels" and of strategy for winning.[1]

The phenomenon most difficult for modern history to explain is the sociocultural process by which collective consciousness shifted from a vision and practice of power appropriate for segmentary societies to a transtribal and even transhistorical vision linking all political power to a divine jurisdiction. The two visions long coexisted, intermingled, and contaminated each other. In practice, struggles for hegemony have always driven the seizure and exercise of power, but theological-juridical discourse, as a result of elaboration, became an autonomous *logosphere* with great capacity to sacralize and transcendentalize state institutions put in place first by the Umayyads in Damascus (661–750) and then by the Abbasids in Baghdad (750–1258). This theological-juridical logosphere, maintained by the ulema, furnished a whole arsenal of concepts and procedures of legitimation that current Islamist movements have revived in their efforts to challenge the powers that be.

It was toward the end of the ninth century that Shi'i and Sunni theorists of authority and power finished elaborating concepts used ever since to account for the stakes of sociopolitical battles fought after the death of Muhammad in 632. The Shi'a developed a maximalist position on the subject of legitimating authority for power; only the descendants or relatives of the Prophet inherited his spiritual charisma and can thus continue to incarnate in history the grace and transcendence manifested in Qur'anic revelation and the teaching of the Prophet. The successors of the Prophet, called Imams,[2] are declared infallible and charged with overseeing in the earthly city the march of all human beings toward eternal salvation.

Sunnis held fast to the fait accompli created by the military victory of the Umayyads in 661. They recognized established authority and developed the idea that unjust government is preferable to generalized disorder. When the Umayyads took power, some Muslims considered them kings (*mulūk*) and not lieutenants of the Prophet (*khulafā'*, or caliphs). The Umayyads did indeed rely upon force rather than the procedures of legitimation introduced by the Prophet in establishing their power. The group known as Khariji (those who go out into combat to defend the cause of God) hung onto the Qur'anic idea that "authority belongs only to God" (*lā ḥukma illā li-llāh*). They were persecuted by the Umayyads and took refuge in North Africa, in the kingdom of Tahert, now Tiaret in Algeria, which was destroyed in 909 by the Fatimid Ismailis. Today we find representatives of this oppositional movement, now known as Ibadi, in the Mzab (Algeria), in Djerba (Tunisia), in the Jabal Nafusa (Libya), and in Oman.

There is not space enough here to detail a long and complex competition in which legitimacy, the attachment of political power to spiritual authority, was at stake. The groups involved in these struggles accomplished an immense task of sacralization and transcendentalization in the form of a theological-religious literature. The most mundane, violent, material conflicts were linked to religious stakes in order to safeguard the idea of continuity, fidelity, and orthodoxy with respect to the founding model supposedly defined in the Qur'an and exemplified by the activity of the Prophet.

As a result, the caliph, for the Sunnis, and even more, the imam, for the Shi'a, became a sacred presence, a simultaneous incarnation of power and authority. Each was to oversee the strict application of the *shari'a*, or Divine Law, which had been sacralized and transcendentalized by the jurist-theologians, drawing upon the science of *uṣūl al-fiqh*, the sources and foundations of law—a highly developed science from the time of Shafi'i (d. 820).

When Khomeini took power in Iran, he brought back to life the whole Shi'i imaginary concerning the authority of the Imam as a case of charismatic legitimation. That event proved that the images constituting the Muslim imaginary about authority in general remained latent and ready for reactivation. It explains the threat brought to bear by all those movements said to be Islamist against regimes they deem too secular and thus too far removed from Islamic legitimacy, which is always linked in the common imaginary to the Medina model.

The abolition of the sultanate by Atatürk did not abolish this imaginary. However, the functions of the caliph or the Imam have undergone sharp deterioration since at least the tenth century. Emirs lacking any tie to the family of the Prophet took power in Baghdad as early as 945 (the Buyids). They left the caliphate in place purely for reasons of legitimation. Various dynasties ruling in various Muslim countries since the tenth century have turned to the ulema in search of legitimation. That is what the Ottoman sultans did from the seventeenth century onward.[3]

Legitimate authority remains a requirement of the common Muslim imaginary, but in historical reality the seizure and exercise of power (*sulṭān*) has usually followed from acts of violence. This is why all regimes established in Muslim countries since the 1950s, with the exception of the Moroccan monarchy, suffer from a deficit of legitimacy. In Arabia the Saʿud family entered into alliance with the Wahhabi religious movement to insure Islamic legitimacy. The ulema still maintain an eminent position in the functioning of monarchical power there.

There has never in the history of Muslim countries been a break in continuity comparable to the French Revolution of 1789–1792, that is, the imposition of a secular and republican imaginary over and against a religious imaginary that had until then held sway in the realm of authority. The overlapping of the religious and the political, of legitimating authority and state power, had been comparable in Christianity to that which emerged in Islam. The new climate created by the French Revolution is now spreading to the Muslim domain, but by indirect means and always hidden by Islamic references destined to reassure the religious imaginary. Demographic growth has considerably loosened the social boundaries of the imaginary in all Muslim societies—a fact that explains why the debate over authority and power is currently so heated and also why it is completely distorted and obstructed by the ideological connivance of states in search of legitimacy and of broad social strata kept away from the corridors of power.[4]

Notes

1. These are examples of religious vocabulary covering, in fact, very precise social groups in Arabia at that time.

2. The word *imām* (imam), which means "guide" or "prayer leader," will be capitalized when referring to the designated successors to the Prophet in the Shiʿa tradition.—TRANS.

3. Note the legal difference indicated by terminology: While the "caliph" is a vicar, an Imam is a charismatic guide, spiritual heir of the Prophet, and a sultan is a holder of power without the procedures and conditions required for a caliph or an Imam.

4. On this question, see my studies in *Pour une critique de la raison islamique* (Paris: Maisonneuve et Larose, 1984) and *Islam: State and Society*, edited by Klaus Ferdinand and Mehdi Mozaffari (London: Curzon, 1988), pp. 53–74.

⚜ 17 ⚜

Judaism, Christianity, and Paganism

What did Islam retain from the previously revealed religions, Judaism and Christianity? And what in addition did it retain from the religions and customs of pre-Islamic Arabia?

*P*osed in this way, these questions are only conceivable within a framework of knowledge characteristic of history as it is written by modern historians. They imply a horizontal window on the time line marking the "evolution" of societies and cultures. This view contrasts with that visible through the vertical window introduced in the Qur'an, and, more generally, in the Hebrew Bible and the New Testament, which reveal that all beings and all events of terrestrial history are dependent on the creative *fiat* of God. The framework for perception of time and space in the Qur'an is mythical; ancient peoples who disobeyed God are evoked from the perspective of salvation history, that is, a perspective that takes account of an eschatological future that goes beyond the chronology of terrestrial events. In this fashion, the pre-Islamic Arab past is categorically dismissed in the Qur'an as an age of darkness and ignorance (*ẓulumāt al-jāhiliyya*), subsequently abolished by the light of Islam (*nūr al-islām*). The pasts of those societies where Islam spread are similarly rejected and condemned to oblivion for their links with paganism.

The Qur'anic position with regard to Judaism and Christianity is obviously different from the Qur'anic view of paganism: Jews and Christians are considered peoples of the Book (*ahl al-kitāb*). Revelation reached them through recognized and venerated prophets such as Abraham and Moses. Jesus, son of Mary, enjoys a special status; he is the Word of God (*kalimatu-llah*) but not the son of God, and he was not crucified. To understand the Qur'anic definition of Jesus the person we must come back to the theological disputes dividing eastern Christians in the fifth and sixth centuries. It took time for the Christian dogma of the Trinity to assert itself in the now familiar standard Catholic form. Current debates between Muslims and Christians do not take account of the historic dimension of the problem. Beliefs elaborated rather late are projected backwards by both sides.

The Qur'an, appearing after the Hebrew Bible and the New Testament, integrates these two other moments of revelation and introduces itself as the final act in the exhibition of the heavenly Book (*al-kitāb*) among human beings. Inversely, the Jews and Christians of Medina refused to recognize Muhammad as a prophet, a fact that explains the split between the communities at the end of the Medina period. There are several conciliatory verses in the Qur'an about the "Sons of Israel" and the Christians, but in Sura 9, revealed in 630 after the taking of Mecca by the believers, the following verses appear. They have served as the basic definition of the legal status of Jews and Christians, who became *dhimmī,* protected peoples:

> Fight those who do not believe in God, even on the Final Day, and who do not proclaim illicit that which God and His Messenger have declared illicit; those who among the people of the Book do not profess the religion of Truth, fight them until they personally pay the *jizya* [tax on non-Muslims], acknowledging their inferiority.
>
> The Jews said: "Othair is the son of God," and the Christians said: "Oint is the Son of God." That is what they say with their own mouths! They repeat what the infidels said before them. May God humiliate them! How they are wrong![1]

These verses, like the rest of Sura 9, warrant a long historical and theological commentary. They have fed an interminable polemic from which there is no escape because it is conducted at the dogmatic level. I cite them here not to touch off new controversies but to attract attention to the urgent need for a modern rereading of these sacred texts that takes account of historical context and doctrinal struggles aggravated by the appearance of the Qur'an at the beginning of the seventh century.

More generally, the comparative history of religions of the Book is still little studied; everyone wants to avoid falling back into medieval polemics. Anything that emphasizes the historicity of sacred texts touches off indignant protest among believers. Only a calm, objective, open brand of history can illuminate declarations such as those quoted above.

History teaches, too, that Islam has retained many of the rites and beliefs characteristic of earlier Arab religion: the rites of pilgrimage to Mecca, the belief in jinn, the mythological representations of ancient peoples, and many edifying tales with clear references to preceding cultures. But the Qur'an recuperated these "ruins of an ancient social discourse" for the construction of a new "ideological palace," as attested by Sura 18, for example.[2] In this sense the Qur'an as a discourse has a mythical structure. Myth refers here to that which the Qur'an calls *al-qaṣaṣ,* a narrative, tale, or story, and not to *usṭūra,* a legend or fable lacking in truth value. By translating myth as *usṭūra* even though the Qur'an furnishes a more useful equivalent, the Arabs have forbidden themselves from thinking about myth and its irreplaceable functions in the construction of the religious imaginary. I emphasize this fact because several readers of my work have falsely interpreted "myth" to mean "fable" or "insubstantial legend"—a definition that destroys the mythical richness of Qur'anic stories.

The utilization in the Qur'an of notions, rites, beliefs, and stories already familiar to previous cultures does not justify a search for "influences" in the style of historicist philologists, who hold a theory of literary or doctrinal creativity that practically rules out any work of synthesis based on widely known materials drawn from ancient traditions. Modern linguistics and semiotics, in contrast, permit us to rediscover the dynamic characteristic of each text, seen from these new viewpoints, as recombining and revitalizing elements borrowed out of context. For every story in the Qur'an, one could show how narrative discourse introduces a new experience of divine thought by pulling names, themes, episodes, and even terms out of previous texts. There are those who have tried to minimize the contribution of the Qur'an by insisting on its "borrowings" from the Hebrew Bible and the New Testament. By doing so they have used the historicist, philological method in the service of a Christian or Jewish apologetic objective. We now know that such an approach is scientifically erroneous.

I would underscore the arbitrary aspect of any historical knowledge based on deliberate refusal to recognize the conditions and contributions characteristic of mythical knowledge. So many misunderstandings between believers, who operate in the mythical framework, and "rationalists," who limit themselves to quantifiable and verifiable space and time, stem from such a refusal. The famous thesis of Taha Hussein on pre-Islamic poetry is an excellent illustration of the divorce between the two types of knowledge. Even today violent clashes and passionate disputes between "Islamists" and historians come out of divergent perceptions of social and cultural reality. I fear that these antagonisms will become more serious as schools spread mythological and highly ideologized images of the past among ever larger populations. Demography has a multiplier effect on the mythologization of religion and the use of history for ideological purposes.

Ideology actually proceeds on the basis of an amalgamation of concepts, notions, historical periods, and levels of meaning, all the while claiming to be highly scientific. Myth, in contrast, always provides food for thought by recapitulating the historic experience of a social group through symbolic expressions, parables, and narrative structures. In the contemporary Muslim context, we can observe a degradation of myth into mythology and ideology, a dilapidation of the symbolic capital bequeathed by Islam, and a reduction of sign into signal. In the languages of the Islamic world, discourse in the sciences of man and society is still too weak and too inadequate to prevent the spread of semantic disorder.

Notes

1. Sura 9, verses 29 and 30.
2. See my *Lectures du Coran* (Paris: Maisonneuve et Larose, 1982). The references are to Claude Lévi-Strauss, *The Savage Mind* (Chicago: University of Chicago, 1966).

⚘ 18 ⚘

The Greek Heritage

Islam acceded to the Greek heritage and transmitted it to the West starting in the twelfth century. Did this opening toward Greek philosophy and science reflect intellectual curiosity on the part of the Muslims of that era, or did it occur at the explicit recommendation of the Qur'an or the Prophet?

Greek philosophy and science experienced rapid growth in the Islamic climate of the eighth and ninth centuries. Neither the Qur'an nor the Prophet encouraged the study of these subjects; quite to the contrary, as early as the ninth century there appeared sharp opposition in Muslim religious circles to the spread of what were said to be the "rational" sciences (*'ulūm 'aqliyya*), as opposed to the religious or traditional sciences (*'ulūm dīniyya* or *naqliyya*). In a celebrated book called *Adab al-kātib,* Ibn Qutayba (d. 889) reacted against those who were always quoting Aristotle.

The success of Greek thought in the region of Iran and Iraq and later in Andalusia can be explained by its implantation in the Near East ever since the conquests of Alexander the Great and its cultivation by the Fathers of the Christian Church from the third century on. Syriac, the language of civilization before Arabic, served as the medium for translation from the Greek; translators, the majority of them Christian, subsequently translated the great works from Syriac and/or Greek into Arabic. The reign of the great caliph Al-Ma'mun (813–833), the founder in Baghdad of the famous House of Wisdom (*dār al-ḥikma*), was the great period of translation. We can then trace a long, winding path from Athens to Baghdad, Rayy, and Cordova by passing chronologically through Alexandria, Antioch, Edessa, and Jundi Shapur in Iran.

This is not the place to report on the complicated and tortuous history of the process of transmission.[1] I will instead concentrate on the lessons to be learned from that great intellectual adventure, which first affected the whole of the Mediterranean region, then the medieval West, and subsequently, with the great discoveries of modern thought, the entire world.

Greek thought represents one of the two great tendencies of reflection and knowledge in the whole Greco-Semitic area. The competing tendency—simultaneously concurrent, complementary, and oppositional—is that of revelation and prophecy. The coming together of these two mental orientations toward the world and knowledge began very early with Flavius Josephus, Philo of Alexandria, Paul, and the other Evangelists. Jews in the Diaspora felt the need to possess a Greek translation of their sacred books. And early Christianity accentuated the movement from Semitic culture (expressed in Hebrew and in Aramaic, Jesus himself having preached in Aramaic) to a culture expressed in Greek. It was a shift in mentality that had important consequences for subsequent developments of Christian theology in both its Roman Catholic and Orthodox Byzantine versions.

In the shift toward Greek culture there were deep splits between Hellenized, Latinized Christianity and Islam, which was still rooted in Semitic soil by Arabic, the language of revelation. The famous debate between the logician Matta ibn Yunus and the grammarian Abū Sa'id al-Sirafi in the tenth century conveys some idea of what was at stake in the philosophical and semantic confrontation between the intellectual magnetism of Greek thought and the spiritual vision of monotheism.[2]

A persistent theme appears in the writings of Church Fathers, neo-Platonists, commentators on Aristotle, Muslim mystics, and Arab and Jewish philosophers of the classical era through Averroës (Ibn Rushd, d. 1198). The work of al-Ghazali (d. 1111), philosopher, theologian, jurist, and mystic, illustrates clearly the intimate interdependence of the conceptual system of philosophy, the legal-theological problematic, and mystic sensitivity. Before him, a famous text circulated under the title *Theology of Aristotle;* in fact, it was an imposture made up of excerpts from *The Enneads* of Plotinus. With the help of a neo-Platonic vocabulary, it was possible to bridge the gap between Aristotelianism and Platonism, on one side, and Jewish, Christian, and Muslim religious thought, on the other. In ethics and logic, the teachings of Aristotle and Plato were absorbed without great resistance; in metaphysics, Hellenized philosophers and theologians (*mutakallimūn*) were divided on three problems: the eternity of the world, the immortality of the soul, and causality. Al-Ghazali and Averroës distinguished themselves in a rich debate on these three questions.

This debate gave rise to two inaccurate portrayals of the fate of philosophy in the Islamic environment. The first was that al-Ghazali put an end to the successes of Greek thought by contributing to the victory of orthodoxy; after the death of Averroës, there was no follow-up to his refutation of al-Ghazali's positions. The second is that Greek philosophical thought, with rationality as its essence, developed brilliantly in the West after the death of Averroës, while what is called illuminative philosophy (*ishrāq*) triumphed in the East after Avicenna (Ibn Sina, d. 1037), Suhrawardi (d. 1234), and Ibn 'Arabi (d. 1240).[3]

These portrayals depend much more on convictions that are essentially religious than on historical inquiries linking the history of ideas, the history of systems of thought, social history, historical psychology, and cultural anthropology. It is easy to understand why few scholars have heretofore managed, or known how, to bring together such diverse and difficult methodologies, problematics, and bodies of knowledge.

As for the fate of philosophy in the land of Islam after Averroës, we must undertake a double historical inquiry comparing sociological conditions for *failure* on the Muslim side with those promoting *success* on the Western, Christian side of what has been called Latin Averroism.

The marginalization and then neglect of philosophy in Islam is but an aspect of the general history of that intellectual domain within Islamic thought designated by the term *ijtihād* in the vocabulary of the jurist-theologians. Intellectual efforts (*ijtihād*) to apply the techniques of exegesis to the Qur'an and the hadith in order to derive legal opinions (*al-aḥkām*) began to diminish in the tenth century. These efforts at creating new approaches gave way to the copying of examplary solutions (*taqlīd*) developed by the learned founders of the great schools of law. Here again we need to study the sociological, ideological, and cultural factors that led very quickly to the victory of "orthodox" reproduction of teachings bequeathed by the competing schools. The history of thought cannot be detached from social history, as I have shown in my book *Arab Humanism in the Tenth Century.*[4] Unfortunately too many Arabic-speaking scholars remain prisoners of an idealist framework for the history of ideas.

Illuminative philosophy must be studied not only from the perspective of historical sociology but also from that of historical psychology—still another dimension ignored by scholars of Islam and Arabism—which concerns social and cultural conditions for the development of the rational and the imaginary, the conscious and the unconscious, dream, dreaming, exoticism, social marginality, psychological structures, psychic forces, and social imaginary. These are contingent elements of a mental reality that historians hardly know how to name correctly; they still tend to reduce them to derisory and misleading contrasts between intrinsic (inner, hidden) meaning and extrinsic (obvious, apparent) meaning (in Arabic, *bāṭin* and *ẓāhir*). Scholarly texts have schematized some of the richest, most complex, most stimulating discussions in all of Islamic thought beneath these two technical headings, *ẓāhir* and *bāṭin*. And the retention of a heresiographic framework that characterizes Ismailis as *bāṭiniyya* and Sunnis as literalists attached to explicit meaning, hence *ẓāhiriyya*, further aggravates the impoverishment of these discussions.

Even today the thought of an Ibn Hazm (d. 1064)—so agile, incisive, daring, and modern—remains poorly known and poorly utilized.[5] The opposition of Maleki jurists to a competitor who extended the linguistic use of the notion of explicit meaning and constructed systems of theology and law that differed from those sustained by "orthodoxy" accounts for this neglect.

These much too hasty remarks are intended to call the reader's attention to the need for contemporary Islamic thought to reinterpret all the great classical works, using several methods and open problematics. Although far from recovering the importance it enjoyed from the eighth to the twelfth centuries, the philosophical outlook is nonetheless indispensable to reaching beyond devastating ideologies that increasingly obstruct all efforts at renewal and creativity.

Apropos of the fate of the philosophy developed in the Islamic lands during the Middle Ages, I must point out another serious gap in knowledge: the indifference and ignorance of Islamic philosophy nurtured incessantly by philosophical teaching in the West. That lacuna compounds the utter rejection philosophy suffered on the Islamic side. In the Middle Ages, however, many philosophical and scientific works were translated from Arabic into Latin; scientific ideas as well as the rationalism of Oxford and the Sorbonne are much indebted to the Arab contribution.

The Arab and Islamic Middle Ages have suffered a much more serious rejection than that accorded the Latin-Christian Middle Ages since the break between philosophy and theology occurred in the sixteenth century. The break was aggravated, of course, by the French Revolution, which laid out a secular, republican imaginary for the West as a whole. That imaginary was disinterested in, if not opposed to, all theological and theocentric visions. The positivism and imperialism of the nineteenth century confirmed this rejection by putting Islam among the backward, even primitive religions—to wit, through the activity of Christian missionaries in the Islamic world. To this date no department of philosophy in any Western university gives any significant attention to the Arab-Islamic phase in the general history of philosophy. The task of directing students in their reading is left to Arabists, most of whom lack philosophical training. Having taught at the Sorbonne since 1961, I can testify to the disinterest of my philosopher colleagues in the teaching of Arab philosophy; likewise, historians of religion remain disinterested in the Islamic case. Beneath such disinterest there lies an old theological and ideological controversy between Islam and the West; an account of it will make a great chapter in psychological history.[6]

The modern perspective on the history of the Mediterranean world opened up so masterfully by Fernand Braudel is still a long way from prevailing on either the Western or the Muslim side. Political struggles and wars of religion have continually divided and disturbed the peoples who inhabit the shores of that sea. We can only hope for a happy and definitive dénouement of the Arab-Israeli war, which continues to delay so many plans, projects, and developments. Its end would at last create opportunities for putting an artificially fragmented cultural space back together again.[7]

The reassembly that I envision spans two major splits both exacerbated by the rivalry of the great powers in the Mediterranean: that between "orthodox" Islamic thought and the philosophical viewpoint, on the one hand, and that between Western thought and religious thought with its Semitic origins, on the other. The juxtaposition of these two historic splits explains why what we call "Islam" and "the West" stand opposed to each other as two poles of knowledge and civilization, even though they sit on the same philosophical-religious pedestal. A rediscovery of this pedestal would permit scholars to once again take up, in a critical way and with better evidence, all those problems repressed in the course of history and amidst the violence of conflict and the emotion of collective imaginaries. Such a path presupposes a thorough revision of curricula in the universities and in primary and secondary schools. This is what is at stake, it seems to me, in an exhaustive history of philosophy and of the religions of the Book in a reunited Western region.

Notes

1. See, for example, Abderahmane Badawi, *La transmission de la philosophie grecque au monde arabe* (Paris: J. Vrin, 1968).

2. See Djamäl Al Amrani, *Bivouac des certitudes* (Paris: SNED, 1968).

3. See Henri Corbin, *En Islam iranien: aspects spirituels et philosophiques,* 4 vols. (Paris: Gallimard, 1971–1972).

4. Mohammed Arkoun, *Humanisme arabe au IVe/Xe siècle,* 2nd ed. (Paris: J. Vrin, 1982).

5. This despite the presentation of his thought by R. Arnaldez in *Grammaire et théologie chez Ibn Hazm de Cordoue* (Paris: J. Vrin, 1956).

6. Normal Daniel began to write that story in *Islam and the West: The Making of an Image* (Edinburgh: Edinburgh University Press, 1960).

7. Arkoun's word is "*remembrement,*" which means "putting back together," as with land that has been subdivided.—TRANS.

✖ 19 ✖

Islam, Science, and Philosophy

What is the relationship among these three orders of intellectual and cultural activity: Islam, science, and philosophy?

$\mathcal{T}$his question is an extension of the one about the Greek heritage but refers more explicitly to the kind of science that is called "exact" or "hard." For the Greeks as for the Arabs in the Middle Ages, science was not separate from philosophy. For Aristotle, physics was linked to metaphysics; similarly, ever since Hippocrates and especially Galen, who was well known to the Arabs, medicine has been an integral part of philosophy. A great work of Avicenna (Ibn Sina) testifies to that fact. But medicine drew in one related discipline after another until it included all the natural sciences, even astronomy. Alchemy flourished but always maintained a relationship to philosophy.[1]

Scientific research does not seem to have encountered religious obstacles in the Islamic domain. The Qur'an persistently invites the faithful to "look at" the created world in order to appreciate the greatness and the power of God. Scientific knowledge of nature, the stars, the heavens, the earth, the flora, and the fauna only reinforces faith and illuminates the symbolic directions of the Qur'an. There exists, moreover, a whole literature of *mirabilia,* the miracles of nature, halfway between scientific observation and religious contemplation of the goodness and power of God.[2]

The Arabs developed mathematics (including algebra, geometry, trigonometry, arithmetic), astronomy, botany, pharmacology, zoology, geography, physiognomy, and psychosomatics, and the West was the beneficiary from the twelfth century on. As in the case of philosophy, this great scientific movement came to a halt not as a result of theological supervision comparable to that exercised by the Christian establishment in the West but rather because of the new social and political environments for knowledge that developed in the whole of the Muslim world starting in the eleventh and twelfth centuries.

Arab-Islamic culture, which matured in the environment of the Umayyad and then the Abbasid empires, was tied to city life. Scholarly activity was concentrated in the great metropolises of Damascus, Baghdad, Isfahan, Cairo, Aleppo, Kairouan, Fez, and Cordova in the shadow of the great princely courts. As long as the empire enjoyed political power and control of trade, a commercial bourgeoisie managed to sustain demand for knowledge and culture; beginning in the eleventh century, when mounting risks threatened the life of the cities already rendered fragile by poorly controlled nomadic and peasant settings, scientific research gave way little by little to the mobilizing discourse of wartime ideology. Against the Reconquista in Spain, the Crusades in Palestine, and the Turkish and Mongol hordes in Iran and Iraq, Muslims needed an orthodox, dogmatic, and rigid but ideologically effective Islam to rally around.

This was the period in which scholastic teaching spread through the *zawāyā,* small mosque schools often run by the religious brotherhoods, and popular religion penetrated the countryside under the guidance of marabouts or local saints. These social and ideological developments radically modified the prospects for scientific and intellectual activity. Narrowing horizons and scholastic hardening accelerated without interruption until the nineteenth century, when a reformist movement appeared in response to colonial pressure. But by then, in about 1830, the historic break with the scientific and cultural legacy of the productive period had been fully consummated. That is why the *salafī* reformists of the late nineteenth century developed a mythological vision of primitive Islam and of the classical civilization it inspired. Mythology, romanticism, and nostalgia for long lost glory left little room for a scientific, critical, constructive approach. The nationalist ideology that emerged to guide the wars of liberation in the twentieth century would only accentuate the semantic break, all the while maintaining the claim to a glorious past, especially on the scientific level. During what is called the liberal age (1850–1940) of the *nahda,* the Arab revival movement, Orientalism, and a few Muslim scholars trained in the philological and historical disciplines spurred scientific research and the publication of some ancient texts, but the work remained insufficient. Thus, the history of science remains less well explored than other topics in Islamic history.

Notes

1. See Paul Kraus, *Jābir Ibn Hayyan: Essai sur l'histoire des idées scientifiques dans l'Islam,* 2 vols. (Paris: 1935, 1942); and E. J. Holmyad, *Alchemy* (Harmondsworth, Eng.: Penguin, 1957).

2. See Zakariya Ibn Muhammad, *'Ajā'ib al-makhlūqāt wa Gharā'ib al-Mawjudat* (Beirut: Dar al-Afaq al Jadida, 1978).

🍃 20 🍃

Sufism

What is the place of Sufism as a doctrinal movement and a style of religious life within Islam? Does Sufism come out of the school of hidden meaning (al-bātiniyya) or the literalist perspective (al-zāhiriyya), a distinction we have already invoked?

*A*ny discussion of Islam that did not devote special attention to its mystical strain called Sufism would be insufficient. This stream of thought is equipped with its own technical lexicon, discourse, and theories. Its style of religious life depends upon rites and ceremonies, individual and collective, that enable both body and soul to participate in the process of incarnating spiritual truths.

The mystical experience develops in every religion; it is not unique to Islam. Historically, it has enjoyed a remarkable continuity, while other modes of religious expression—theology, law, exegesis, architecture, and institutions—have undergone more rapid change.

The ultimate purpose of mysticism is, first and foremost, a lived experience of an internal, unifying encounter between believer and his or her personal God (the sense of the infinite and the absolute linked to the divine as taught by all religions). This experience is analyzed as it is formalized through examination of consciousness, through the mystic's turning in on the self. Once reflected upon in this way and put into writing, the experience serves to nourish aspiring disciples (*murīdūn*), who set themselves upon a mystical course (*sulūk*) under the guidance of a master (*shaykh*).

Mystical contemplation is an individual exercise, independent of the worship practiced by the community; it is lived as a gratuitous gift of God, which is reciprocated by the loving gift of the mystic. Islam encourages communication with God without the mediation of priests. In the view of legal-theological orthodoxy, however, mystics go too far in their ritual detachment from the community, especially when they reach the stage of ecstatic unity (*al-waḥda*) with God. When the great mystic al-Hallaj, who was tortured in 922, uttered the famous theopathic phrase, "*anā-l-ḥaqq*," "I am God-Truth," he met with incomprehension from literalists and ritualists, who would not admit that the human "I" could be unified to the same extent as the divine, transcendent "I." "We are two minds poured into a single body," said al-Hallaj. This assertion earned him the accusation of incarnation, *ḥulūl*. Louis Massignon, the great authority on al-Hallaj and practitioner of dialectics and ecstatics, wrote: "Hallaj tried to reconcile dogma and Greek philosophy with the rules of mystical experimentation. He was a precursor of al-Ghazali in that respect."[1]

Massignon's assessment of al-Hallaj underscores the richness and originality of mysticism from the seventh to the ninth centuries in a society where several cultural traditions and currents of thought originating in ethnocultural groups (*mawālī*) converged. Philosophy was capable of unraveling a mystical or ascetic experience, just as mysticism could open itself to philosophy. The theologian and the jurist could be drawn to both philosophy and Sufism. Such interchanges of ideas and exchanges of experience could occur in cosmopolitan cities such as Baghdad, Basra, Rayy, Mecca (as a result of the pilgrimage), and Cairo.

Mystics of the formative period succeeded in remaining solidly rooted in the intellectual terrain of their time, all the while suspending their consciousness of time and the world of objects and edging toward an existential monism (*waḥdat al-wujūd*, in the words of the great mystic Ibn 'Arabi, d. 1240). They described their experience with a style and an acuity of analysis that even now attract the attention of all students of religious psychology as well as practitioners of the mystical way. I will mention the names of Hasan al-Basri (d. 772), Muhasibi (d. 857), Bistami (d. 874), and Junayd (d. 910).[2]

One cannot neglect the social and political aspects of the mystical movement if one is to understand the tensions generated by great innovators such as al-Hallaj. The ready-made clientele for mystics is clearly an impoverished urban milieu consisting of the members of marginal social categories and those who cannot rise into the privilege of the leisured classes of merchants, landowners, and "intellectuals" associated with the exercise of power or protected by patrons. Mysticism's relationship with the working classes evolved after the eleventh century toward an association with the society's more dangerous, contentious classes (*futūwa, 'ayyārūn*). Then, in a later stage, from the thirteenth through the nineteenth centuries, local saints (marabouts) were associated with the rural and mountain populations whom central authorities could not control, as in the Maghrib toward the end of the Merinid dynasty. In that period mysticism became a highly diverse movement of religious brotherhoods, expressing and crystallizing tribal and clan rivalries in rituals and ceremonies unique to each brotherhood. Throughout the Muslim world, brotherhoods worked to gain prestige, followers, and political ground by sending trained marabout missionaries into teaching centers. Each such center, or *zāwiya*, was linked to a founding saint. Everywhere the holy emanations (*baraka*) of the saints worked miracles to win the confidence of populations, whose illiteracy and foreignness to Arabic, as in the case of the Berbers in the Maghrib and of Africans south of the Sahara, rendered them all the more credulous.

This is the Islam of the marabouts, dominated by the work of saints and the constant diffusion of holiness, that a conquering, positivistic West discovered in all the Muslim countries in the nineteenth century. Interpretations and misunderstandings emanating from this situation continue to feed the Western imaginary of Islam even now.

In the current context of Muslim societies, it is difficult to assess precisely the significance of what wrongly continues to be called Sufism. Like Islam as a whole, the shape of Sufism depends upon the cultural system and the political regime where it manifests itself. The powerful movement toward ideologization already mentioned with regard to Islam clearly affects Sufism, too, especially since nation-states are wary of any resurgence of saint cultures and careful to keep watch over the places and milieus hospitable to brotherhoods. In certain cases, as in Senegal, brotherhoods become pillars of support and transmission belts for the power of the state, which accords them privileges in exchange. For these reasons, sociological surveys aiming to identify links or conflicts between militant Islam and the Islam of the brotherhoods are difficult if not impossible to carry out. The Sufi milieu does not lend itself to surveys; theirs is a silent, discrete Islam. One would love to know more about its spirituality and about its ties to the intellectual concerns of classical Sufism. Political analysts err in concentrating all their attention on the burning, militant Islam in plain sight; other manifestations of Islam deserve to be more closely examined and better known to the public at large.

Many Westerners convert to Islam these days by means of what is introduced to them as Sufism. The psychocultural complex at work in such conversions deserves to be studied in relation to the outcasts produced by a Western society deemed cold, rationalist, materialist, and without ideals. There are many illusions, mistakes, hasty judgments, and misunderstandings on one side and the other, just as there are for infatuations with the religions of India and, more generally, with the multiplication of Christian sects in the West. These phenomena show the extent to which contemporary scientific thought as well as political authorities fail to take account of religious movements, channel them, and assure them adequate room for expression. Society is content to marginalize the sects and stigmatize religious and cultural deviance without seriously reexamining the spiritual dimension of human existence through the multiple experiences recorded in the history of religions.

Currently Islam cannot claim superiority in that regard. Where there are manifestations of the "spiritual" in Muslim societies, it is more a result of the survival of social structures and subsistence economics conducive to the manifestation of traditional religion than of a more effective resistance on the part of Islam to the disruptions generated by the modern economy and industrial civilization. The output of theological or mystical goods does not compare with that which once energized and enriched classical Islam. That is why people are reusing ancient works in contemporary contexts.

The fact that mystical experiences as described and taught by the ancients elicit disciples in our societies, deeply troubled at every level of their existence, only demonstrates the capacity of these societies to produce cultural and psychological marginality. Of course, the ancient testimony contains aspirations toward the transcendence of social and cultural context. Still, the experience of the divine can no longer seek support in symbolic capital, a sense of miracle, a mythical universe, and a capacity for bewitchment. All such assets have been neatly destroyed not only by our surroundings of concrete, factories, and public housing but by a replacement myth of secular and republican origin characteristic of our current societies.

The so-called Islamist movements combat this myth, which came out of the English, American, and especially the French revolutions of the seventeenth and eighteenth centuries. But political regimes, state structures, systems of production and exchange, generalized corruption, technological culture, destruction of the semiological environment, dilapidation of traditional symbolic capital, loss of bewitchment, and sacredness of time and place all give a priori shape to modern sensitivities and the framework of modern perceptions. They derive from a myth of secular, "republican" origin. (Republics, understood as democratic regimes, exist in only a formal sense in most Muslim countries, but authority there, whether monarchical or formally republican, is oriented toward the general secularization of society.)

I have already suggested that the line of demarcation between intrinsic and extrinsic cannot be drawn between internal and external, between that which is *hidden* and can be known only via initiation and that which is *apparent* or *manifest*, which is immediately accessible to sight or reason. Traditional Islamic thought psychologized, in the framework of a gnostic culture, a psycholinguistic reality that we describe today in terms of deep and superficial structures, implicit and explicit discourse in language. Ancient practitioners of exegesis encountered this distinction in trying to decipher Qur'anic discourse. The notions of *taqdīr* and *taḍmīn* (implied, implicit) and of explicit, but either clear or ambiguous, verses requiring more analysis or greater interpretative effort (*muḥkamāt, mutashābihāt*) put them on the path toward distinguishing between what is said and unsaid and understanding what is said by way of the unsaid. All the same, their theory of language and the relations between language and thought lacked an adequate approach to metaphor and metonymy, any recognition of myth as the key to a mode of knowledge, and any conception of symbol and sign as fundamental elements of signification in all semiological systems and especially in this sort of religious discourse from which so many other systems of signification are derived.

The ancients were of course familiar with metaphor, metonymy, parable, edifying story, and sign-symbols. (The word for verse in the Qur'an is *āya,* a "sign" or "mark.") They commonly used all the tools of expression in all the semiological systems they produced. (Mystical discourse is one; there were others for dress, furniture, architecture, urbanism, legal codes, and so on.) But they could not take full account of the role played by each of these rhetorical, linguistic, and semiological tools in organizing all signification. Scholars are only beginning to glimpse, for example, the capacity of metaphor, symbol, and myth to establish meaning with regard to the construction of the imaginary and the historical avatars of meaning. Meaning is no longer stable, forever rooted in transcendence, but is rather exposed to the continual genesis of destruction. Meaning is generated by semantic creativity, the inventiveness of the subject under the pressure of new existential demands that necessitate destroying, transforming, or surpassing previous meanings. The process entails the existence of live, dead, and revived metaphors or the degradation of symbols into simple signs or even into signals that are merely descriptive.

Mystical discourse amplifies, develops, and utilizes the symbolic and mythical part of founding religious discourse (the Qur'an for Sufism, the New Testament for Christians, the apocalyptic texts for Jewish cabala) to construct an initiating knowledge, a gnosticism that sustains the mystic journey and finds itself enriched in return by the data of every experience carried to its conclusion. Scholars thus dispose of particularly rich bodies of work for the study of semantic and symbolic eruptions in language under the pressure of intense, internal spiritual experience and, inversely, of the capacity generated in the course of mystical experiences for renewal and revival of articulated discourse. Louis Massignon perceived this decisive importance of language very well in studying the "technical lexicon of Muslim mysticism" and in translating the *Diwān* of al-Hallaj.

To complete this inquiry I would have to show how the spiritual contents of mystical discourse are translated and incorporated into the flow of normal religious exercises through rites, prayers, recitations, performances, and corporal disciplines. The genesis and functions of what we call "faith" are surely linked to these linguistic and psychophysiological mechanisms. We now know that language training takes place through the reception of sounds corresponding to phonological structures. Deaf mutes use skin and bones for the reception of these sounds. Units of sound are imprinted in the neuronic system as if on tape; their faithful reproduction is thus assured. This does not, of course, eliminate the creativity of the subject, which resides in variable abilities to formulate new combinations at the moment of semantic and symbolic eruption. The highest degree of such creativity is to be found in prophets and great artists.

Notes

1. Louis Massignon, *The Passion of al-Hallaj: Mystic and Martyr of Islam,* 4 vols. (Princeton: Princeton University, 1982).

2. See A. J. Arberry, *Sufism: An Account of the Mystics of Islam* (London: Allen and Unwin, 1969); Annemarie Schimmel, *Mystical Dimensions of Islam* (Chapel Hill: University of North Carolina, 1975).

ॐ 21 ॐ

The Person

How is the notion of the person presented in Islamic thought?

*E*veryone in the West knows how much media attention Muslims receive in Western countries and is familiar with the tone and the imagery—ancient in origin but enriched every day—that serves to feed a powerful Western imaginary of this far-off world, so different, hostile, violent, and backward yet so very near both geographically and even socially.

In Muslim societies themselves, news of these same events is not any more objective, open, or positive than in the West. Rather, the news is carefully controlled by states anxious to guarantee their survival and legitimacy. Islam is thus used as an ideological lever, a tool of offensive or defensive justification, and is very rarely a subject of study or a source of value certainty in the fight against aspects of underdevelopment such as ignorance, eruptions of violence, corruption, and intolerance.

What sort of responses, what states of mind do thinkers, scholars, artists, the political class—in short, the political and intellectual elites—bring to this overwhelming state of affairs, to urgent demands issued in highly unstable societies and amidst increasing semantic disorder?

I distinguish classic Islamology from applied Islamology to demonstrate methodological and epistemological classifications, not an irreducible contrast between two applications of a single discipline. Roughly speaking, classic Islamology looks exclusively at texts deemed a priori to represent a religious tradition, a mode of thought, a culture, and a civilization. Classic texts produced between the seventh and thirteenth centuries have long been the object of scholarly attention, and they continue to get privileged attention, since the first phase of exploration, even discovery, is far from ended. Many manuscripts, indeed, have not yet been published or even discovered. In this sense, *classic* Islamology remains an indispensable exercise.

The choice of texts as handholds for understanding Islam and Muslim societies becomes more debatable and dangerous when one reaches the contemporary period, the nineteenth and twentieth centuries, and particularly the effervescent history of the years since 1947. And the readings generally given to these texts mislead as much as they enlighten what is really at stake in the developments under way, the forces at work, the collective ambitions, and the guidelines prescribed for these societies. This is where *applied* Islamology assumes its full significance and becomes a scientific necessity. The inevitable problems of a philological interpretation do not, of course, arise for contemporary texts as they do for medieval texts.

I have chosen the theme of the person to illustrate, with the help of a particularly rich example, the methods and epistemological positions required of an approach to Islam that combines what classic Islamology has established with the lines of questioning, the procedures of analysis, and the practical purposes of applied Islamology. To introduce the study of such a subject, I will consider the following three questions:

1. How does the problem of the person explode into a reality that cannot be sidestepped in contemporary Muslim societies?
2. What intellectual equipment and scientific and cultural resources are available to contemporary Islamic thought as it seeks new answers that respect both the incontrovertible teachings of the tradition and the undeniable imperatives of modernity?
3. How are we to situate the "Islamic" response to the problem of the person among the conceptions and specific viewpoints assigned by modern scientific thought? Posed in this way, the question will force us to engage in a radical critique of the hegemonic position of Western thought, which, through its scientific and technological advancement, seems likely to govern the fate of the person for a long time to come.

"The person is a contradiction incarnate of individual and sacral, form and matter, indefinite and finite, liberty and destiny."[1] This rich definition shows that the notion of the person cannot be approached without recourse to several disciplines. Social and legal history must come first, for it is the social and legal order that makes a person as such and not otherwise; psychology, sociology, anthropology, philosophy, and in the case of the great religious traditions, theology, come afterwards.[2]

On the Islamic side, the theme of the person appears in several strains of classic thought. One cannot, however, be content with looking at religious, ethical, legal, and philosophical frameworks bequeathed by speculative Islamic thought; rather, one must undertake a process of critical reflection, starting from a consideration of the new circumstances of historical development prevailing in Muslim societies since the 1950s.

In a previous study,[3] I showed how demographic pressures; the introduction of an industrial economy; the emergence of an authoritarian, autonomous state separate from civil society and even opposed to it; increasing dependence with regard to modern technology; cultural backwardness; dramatic departures from ecological realities; and terrorism by peasants, mountain people, and nomads have come together to alter radically the circumstances for the emergence and development of the person.

Introduced everywhere with great ideological fervor, agrarian revolutions have stripped from the peasant world and desert civilization the ecological, territorial, and agrarian foundations of a code of honor (*'ird*) that had functioned for millennia. Independent states conducted operations of nomad resettlement with a degree of destructive aggressiveness to be explained only by the utter ignorance of the nomad world to be found in ministerial technocracies. Before and after the advent of Islam, this code of honor functioned to maintain order in each group: The internalization of the value system culminating in honor permits each individual to raise himself to ever higher ranks (*afḍal, faḍl, 'ayn, a'yān*) and to exercise an authority appropriate to the person. This was an authority of the mind over other minds involving the free acquiescence of conscience to the values incarnated and practiced by the master, chief, or wise man (*sayyid, shaykh, imām, mahdī, wāli,* or marabout).

The code of honor in traditional societies is unwritten; it is lived and internalized in the form of habits that order individual and collective behavior. It is not transmitted by theoretical teaching but instead reproduced through daily life in all its formal, ritual, social, and symbolic complexity. Descriptions involving the most diverse and widely dispersed sorts of groups[4] show the importance of the ethnological approach and the anthropological problematic in the study of the status of the person in the Islamic domain. Islam has certainly introduced change by the imposition of a centralizing state, a written culture to compete everywhere with the oral tradition, and a law entailing conflicts with local customs. But the sociological extension of these tools for the "domestication" of "wild" societies has been limited by resistance to the sociohistorical model condemned by the Qur'an under the *jāhiliyya* label. The term has been taken up by contemporary militants such as Sayyid Qutb in Egypt for the designation of societies gone astray under the dominion of illegitimate, anti-Islamic powers.

Classic Islamology has paid little attention to this fact, which is critical to the understanding of Muslim societies both past and present. By completely separating the inquiries of historicist philology from investigations appropriate to ethnography, ethnology, and anthropology, classic Islamology limited itself instead to learned texts and fashioned an ideal version of Islam consistent with that of Muslim theologians and jurists themselves.

One cannot identify the status and functions of the person without beginning from a sociology of Islamic law. In a single society such as Egypt, Saudi Arabia, Indonesia, or Turkey, Muslim law is not applied equally for all groups or classes coexisting in the same social space. Bedouin law, Berber law, Kurdish law—all tied to local knowledge—have long resisted the will of the Muslim state to wipe out once and for all the sectors of "rebellion," such as the *blād al-siba* in Morocco.

The degree to which the Arab language and culture have penetrated a society also determines the types of persons who emerge in each sociocultural milieu. In Kabylia, that highly populated region of northern Algeria, neither Muslim law nor Arabic and Arab culture prevailed before independence in 1962. The version of Islam propagated by marabouts necessarily assimilated and consecrated the local code of honor and a symbolic capital that proved especially resistant to outside influence. The same thing can be said of Moroccan and Libyan Berbers and of numerous other African groups.

Nationalist governments, products in most cases of wars of liberation waged during the 1950s, fought savagely against ethnocultural and confessional distinctions, which constituted obstacles to national unity and hence to the stabilization and diffusion of central power. There was no exception to this political voluntarism, which, already in Turkey under Atatürk in the 1920s, wanted to end distinctions, geographical dispersion, superstition, popular religion, and mystical movements—all those things, in short, that made the code of honor effective in society and hence imparted strength to the person trained according to this code in "wild" society.

This implacable struggle between "wild" and "tame" societies had already begun with the Prophet in Mecca and Medina. It received not only exemplary ideological expression in the Qur'an but also an "ontological" foundation for the transcendentalization of an essentially anthropological dichotomy. The Qur'an, and all subsequent Islamic thought, is vehement in contrasting the "shadows of the *jāhiliyya*" with the "light of Islam." The *jāhiliyya* was the phase of history in which human beings had not yet received revelation: They lacked the true knowledge (*'ilm*) taught by God whereby believers could modify their actions in the prospect of eternal salvation. Islam is the eruption of this *'ilm* to guide the faithful toward salvation.

In terms of social and cultural anthropology, the *jāhiliyya* is Arab society together with its code of honor before the advent of Islam. Islam succeeded in establishing new symbolic capital and a new eschatological horizon, but values in the code of honor were preserved and even sacralized, ontologized, and transcendentalized by the discourse of revelation. With its commitment to the faith and to fighting (jihad) for the Prophet's cause, the small group of early believers (*mu'minūn*) took on the development of the Muslim "person" and thus of a similarly Muslim society. The model for the training of the person in Islam, the religion's capacity to span all cultural frontiers, its irrepressible recurrence in situations of social and ideological effervescence, and its current growth despite the challenge of industrial civilization can all be explained by four decisive factors:

1. the normative character and mythical structure of Qur'anic discourse;
2. the staying power and provocative force of religious ritual through which are realized the semantic contents and flights of eschatological hope introduced and amplified by Qur'anic discourse;
3. the establishment and persistence of a centralizing state, which took "true religion" (orthodoxy) under its protection and drew legitimacy from it in return; and
4. the installation in the founding phase of Islam (610–632) of a political-religious imaginary that would subsequently assimilate "orthodox" representations of primitive Islam and produce a universal "Islamic" history intended to be seen as the application of models initiated by the Prophet for individual and collective behavior.

One can never overemphasize the role and recurrent power of the politico-religious imaginary put in place by what I have called the Medina experience. All historical activity of any significance in the Islamic domain has been a result of this imaginary. These activities themselves presuppose the production of a type of person who has internalized all the representations, all the ideal symbolic images carried by traditional Islamic discourse.

One could rewrite the whole history of societies inheriting this model of activity to demonstrate the constant interaction between the politico-religious imaginary shared by all the faithful and the analytical, conceptual, and logical reasoning of intellectuals. The latter tried to introduce rational coherence into a domain already occupied by versions of the official discourse of the "Islamic" state or by competing forms of discourse better adapted to local symbolic codes. Thus, as Lila Abu-Lughod has shown quite well, two forms of discourse coexist among the Awlad 'Ali of Egypt's western desert. One, personal, expresses intimate values and is employed exclusively within restricted circles (the young, relatives). The other, public, exalts common values of the group. As a result, the person takes shape and asserts himself or herself at two separate levels according to the mode and place of expression but also integrates the two systems of values, which define and support the group.[5]

Two other sorts of more general discourse were eventually superimposed on the Awlad 'Ali's own pair, as they were on other ethnocultural groups in the area broadly termed "Muslim." One was the Islamic discourse common to the whole tradition produced by the Medina experience. This discourse has been taken up again and widely propagated ever since the 1930s by the Islamist movements. The second was the official discourse of the nationalist state, which propagated secular values borrowed from the West with respect to the economy and political institutions.

How were these competing forms of discourse organized? How were they articulated? And in what ways were they mutually exclusive? The person should be studied as a haven of liberty; choices are made, options eliminated, and combinations put together to make up each *personality* and eventually to confirm the *selection* of the personage, the leader, the imam at the level of the local group, the nation, and the community of believers. Such a study becomes indispensable to a reconstruction of the delicate mechanisms that definitively order both individual destinies and the historical development of societies.

In light of these observations, one could compose a series of portraits that would make it possible to explain the conditions for the appearance and influence or, to the contrary, for the disappearance and failure of the "great men" of each society. Moreover, with the help of the Islamic example, one could revive the concept of *basic* personality launched not long ago by Abram Kardiner[6] but left behind by anthropologists.[7]

What sort of philosophy of the person is implied and prescribed by personages such as Bourguiba, Hassan II, Boumediene, Nasser, Qadhdhafi, Saddam Hussein, Hafiz al-Asad, Zia ul-Haq, and Khomeini—leaders who weigh so heavily upon the history of Muslim societies today?

It is not enough to describe general conceptions, the circumstances of accession to power, the methods of government, and the popularity of these leaders. We must know the cultural and social genesis of their personalities and the intimate convictions they hold as private persons. The distance between the private and public personages would then measure the effective capacity of the person to create and incarnate the values advanced by the society and, inversely, expose the limitations or constraints imposed by the society on the emancipating initiative of the person.

To complete, correct, and consolidate this survey of leaders, one would have to add studies of the members of another group of persons chosen from civil society. The more a state is authoritarian—that is, an anonymous force that represses or ignores the hopes of civil society—the more counterpersonalities, counterleaders whose complaints, protests, and propositions refer to another philosophy of the person, arise from the depths of that society. Frequently evoked examples include militant figures such as Sayyid Qutb, theorist of the Muslim Brothers who was executed under Nasser in 1966; the blind shaykh 'Abd al-Hamid Kashk, imam of the 'Ayn al-Hayat Mosque in Cairo, where he has delivered sermons that stir popular fervor beyond the borders of Egypt (via the very broad distribution of cassettes in the Arabic-speaking world); 'Abd al-Salam Faraj, author of *The Neglected Duty* and theorist of the movement al-Jihad, which assassinated Sadat in 1981; Hasan al-Turabi, head of the Muslim Brothers in the Sudan; Abu 'Ali al-Mawdudi, marshal of Pakistani Muslims, whose teachings have leaped across all boundaries in the Muslim world; 'Ali Shari'ati, who helped to energize the revolutionary movement in Iran; Shukri Mustafa, organizer of Tafkir Wal-Hijra;[8] and Rashid Ghannouchi, one of the leaders of the Islamic Tendency Movement in Tunisia. One could extend indefinitely the list of these movements of protest and violent action. The names often evoke an ambitious program of return to the "true Islam," as do Islamic Jihad, the Party of Allah, Islamic Justice, and the Youth of Muhammad.

Although these movements scarcely receive broad public support, their discourse expresses quite appropriately the disappointed expectations, the sentiments of frustration, oppression, and anguish, and the need for hope among the young generations born after 1950. These young people were born and have grown up in an atmosphere dominated by wars of liberation and the euphoric phase of national rebirth; subsequently they have experienced the enormous disappointments of defeat in 1967, the retreat of the great Arab nation exalted by Nasser, the destruction of liberties, the negation of human rights, imperialist appetites, disorderly development, the ineffectiveness and often the destructiveness of traditional values, unemployment, urban congestion, unequal distribution of resources, waste, and corruption. The progress achieved in public health, free schooling (but not education), security, transportation, and domestic comfort cannot compensate for the damages to the person caused by the destruction of ecological, sociological, and agrarian structures in which the ancestral values confirmed and sacralized by Islam were rooted. These structures included systems of blood relations, rules for supervising the distribution of goods, and matrimonial strategies.

Between leaders in power together with technocrats who surround them and counterleaders who aspire to power, between official culture and the counterculture of protest movements, there is the world of the intellectuals, more or less affected by modernity, and the world of the ulema, who try to keep their monopoly on the management of religious values. These two social groups play roles that cannot be neglected in defining conditions for the training, self-fulfillment, and alienation of the person. The ulema and the intellectuals most often let themselves be pulled in the wake of the state; they are, in fact, employed by the state and paid by the state; they are restrained, as a result, by an obligation to be discreet if not to be explicitly committed to serve an ideology of legitimation. The traditional ulema's function of critique, employing theological and moral censure, has been completely abandoned. The intellectuals, seduced by the independence of their Western counterparts, choose exile or self-censure, or they seek official recognition, which they justify by the need of any society for access to points of "scientific" reference. In the chronological phase extending from independence into the present, no Muslim society has permitted a group of independent, critical intellectuals to emerge from their shells, make themselves known, and engage in continuous activity—certainly not a group influential enough to represent that *standard* of authority indispensable to the flowering of the person. Via a "debt of meaning," a person becomes a consciousness obliged to communicate with other units of consciousness, all deferring to the authority of constraining truth.[9] It is still difficult to find the sort of intellectual, whether artist or leader, who affirms, protects, and defines the destiny of the person as the point and ultimate concern of all philosophy.

It is no doubt risky and dangerous to petition against this decision or that policy of a government. Intellectuals have been arrested and imprisoned for trying to defend human rights in those very countries where such a defense constituted the very essence of the struggle for national liberation. But one must go beyond political explanations for the timidity of intellectuals to consider, as well, a serious phenomenon of breakdown within Islamic consciousness; I will come back to that topic. Let's keep in mind for now that the distinctive ethos of Islamic consciousness is its relationship to the absoluteness of God, experienced in the ritual repetitions required by canonical obligations, meditation on the Word of God, contemplation of the work of God in the universe and in its creative, joyous obedience to the law, relegation of reason to the role of servant, and radical refusal of any polytheism, which would relativize God and end the search for the absolute.

What remains of this ethos, the moral and the spiritual intent, in the consciences of those devoted to the implacable quest for power—political, economic, or cultural? Or in the conduct of the middle classes, avid for social promotion? Or in the imaginary of those who militate for the installation of an "authentic" Islamic regime? Does there exist a realm of authority that a person can draw upon as a resource and employ to test the validity and significance of the values that underpin authority and compel respect for it in society? Does Islamic thought today have the indispensable intellectual and cultural means, the freedoms, and the social cadres to promote a *modern* philosophy of the person?

There has long been talk about the economic and social underdevelopment of the Third World, but there has not been the same attention given to cultural backwardness, which has been dramatically accentuated by the imposition of Western models for all that pertains to material modernity. All Muslim societies suffer these days from the consequences of the disparity between the frenetic demands that feed consumer civilization and the refusal or even repression of intellectual and cultural modernity. Recently built universities in several countries, particularly in those richest in foreign exchange such as Saudi Arabia or Algeria, furnish a striking illustration of the divorce between the demand for material modernity—fanciful architecture, well-equipped laboratories for the "exact" sciences, openness to technology and industrial production—and mistrust of the human and social sciences. Islam as a religion remains a preserve of the schools of theology and traditional universities like Al-Azhar in Cairo, Al-Zitouna in Tunis, and al-Qarawiyyin in Fez. All these schools have long professed a desire to modernize, but they remain guardians of "Islamic orthodoxy," the places where it is reproduced. The animators of the Islamist movements come there to forage.

The very use of the expression "Islamic thought" has become problematic because ordinary Islamic discourse, essentially ideological and apologetic, with its schemas, its postulates, its references, and its semantic disorder, has prevailed even among the ulema and intellectuals, who are supposed to take up, defend, protect, and enlarge. They are supposed to renew the critical capacity and creative reflection so richly illustrated by classic thinkers. Efforts at integrating intellectual modernity into a brand of thought that does its best to merit the label "Islamic" do exist, but they are the product either of persons who are isolated and dispersed in the West or of persons who are unknown, little known, or objects of violent protest within their own countries.

From concession to concession, from tactical surrender to the internalization of the "values" carried by the common imaginary, intellectuals affected by modern criticism are induced to mistake the necessities of nation building and hence ideological commitment for the primacy of properly intellectual, cultural, and spiritual efforts to promote, protect, and exercise the *right of the mind to truth*. Opportunities for the affirmation and development of the person reside in this fundamental distinction.

This discussion touches upon a central difficulty of the human and social sciences: Out of concern for objectivity, a scholar declines to intervene as a person whose destiny is at risk in any action aimed at knowing. When the object of study is religious knowledge, the scholar rarely finds a satisfactory position between partisanship and reductive analysis. The emotional climate that predominates in Muslim societies today renders the scientific study of a large number of delicate problems impossible.

What is the actual status of the person when the right to think, to express oneself, and to publish, sell, and buy writings of all sorts is strictly supervised by the ministry of information or of "national guidance"? The expression "the right of the mind to truth" may appear pompous or derisory to a Westerner accustomed to enjoy full freedom in the intellectual and cultural domain. But for a Muslim the struggle for this right always takes place within dogmatic closure. I recall in this respect the fight of the philosophers to loosen the hold of the theologian-jurists on the exercise of reason. Ultimately, orthodoxy overcame the "rational sciences," which it termed intrusive (*dakhīla*).

Nationalist ideology and the demand for a return to a mythical version of Islam today exercise the same sort of pressure on scientific rationality as did the legal-theological teaching of the Middle Ages. So-called Islamic thought has never engaged in reflection on the ideological function of religious discourse. As a result, assertions derived from the Qur'an are uniformly taken as truth so long as they are guaranteed by the experts who founded the great schools of interpretation or by the ulema deemed to be authorities by the consensus of believers.

The person trained inside this dogmatic closure cannot think about the problem of ideology. Such a person will, quite to the contrary, absorb as totally true a text such as *The Neglected Duty* (*Al-farīda al-ghā'iba*), which I shall examine shortly. I will retain from the outset this principle of interpretation: that ideological deviation occurs within the framework of Islamic thought each time that an author, echoing more or less faithfully a school, a community, or a tradition, transforms Qur'anic discourse from an *open* into a *closed* cognitive system.

By invoking the existence of a Qur'anic discourse that is cognitively open, I am not falling back into the dogmatic closure I have been warning about. I envisage the Qur'an as a linguistic space where several types of discourse (prophetic, legislative, narrative, sapiential) work simultaneously and intersect each other. Purely linguistic and semiotic analysis[10] serves to distinguish the existence of a central mythical structure calling upon symbol and metaphor to confer potential meanings on all Qur'anic enunciations, which are constantly made actual in recurrent existential situations.

The contrast between closed and open is not speculative or an act of faith. It can be verified linguistically and historically by revealing the constant interaction of language, history, and thought—three realms for the production of meaning. The reading of the Qur'an requires us to join the three realms, which are customarily explored separately by specialists: linguists, historians, and philosophers.

Replete with these suggestions, let's see what *The Neglected Duty* can teach us about the workings of Islamic thought and about the person who turns there for principles of thought and life. This text poses forcefully the problem of the person from the viewpoint of today's militant Islam. It is, in fact, the work of Muhammad 'Abd al-Salam Faraj, who was executed on April 15, 1982, with others accused of assassinating President Sadat. In *The Neglected Duty,* the author prescribes jihad—armed combat against the infidels to assure the full, continuous, no-concessions-made application of the revealed law—as the basic premise for the reestablishment of an "Islamic" government in Egypt and elsewhere. The central argument is thus a justification for the assassination of any person who, like President Sadat, establishes a regime contrary to the law.

Moreover, this text has, with good reason, been presented and widely analyzed by Western Islamicists as a contribution to the understanding of Islamic radicalism's vision of the world. In addition to the brief comments of Gilles Kepel in *The Prophet and the Pharaoh,*[11] Johannes J.G. Jansen has provided an English translation and a long introduction to the text. The translator emphasizes that "no one reading the text of *The Neglected Duty* can fail to be struck by its *coherence* and the force of its *logic.*"[12]

But he does not specify the type of coherence and logic employed to impress the reader; nothing is said either about the cognitive system that orders the workings of discourse and permits a wide reception by the Muslim public.

One should note that the impression made on the Western reader is quite the opposite of "holy" fervor elicited in the Muslim reader or listener. A Westerner is uneasy, even distressed, at the "logic" of a faith that shows disdain for a conception of the person that compels the respect of everyone in a Western state under the rule of law. For a Muslim looking at the text, faith suffers before the "tyrants" who have substituted their arbitrary laws for the judgment of God. Western Islamicists have observed this difference in perception and have dug a gulf between the Western vision of the person and the terrifying vision of *Radical Islam*,[13] reinforcing in this way the conviction that the West must eventually be prepared to contain the violence of militant Islam.

I want to engage in some radical thinking in order to get beyond this dichotomy, which is essentially theological, metaphysical, apologetic, and ideological in varying degrees according to the emphases of particular authors on one or another of the multiple aspects of such a comparative study. This desire is a further reason for me to take my turn at reading the manifesto of the assassins of Sadat.

Jansen lays out the sources on which the text is based, the political and social circumstances for its appearance, and the psychological efficacy of its protests, promises, and affirmations. What remains to be done is to evaluate the status of the text from the viewpoint of an epistemological critique, not only of its method or its problematics but, more important, of the cognitive system on which the "coherence" and "logic" are founded. Such work must be done in two parts, first using the rules and principles of criticism employed by classical Islamic thought and then with the rules and principles of modern epistemological critique. By subjecting Islamic thought to modern criticism, I aim to integrate it into the general flow of consciousness and elicit its position on the status of the person, not on the basis of "orthodox" presuppositions or some version of Western philosophy but within the perspective of a general critique of the person considered as a value.

To interpret the whole of the text would require a book still thicker than Jansen's.[14] The ideological orientation of *The Neglected Duty* emerges from a sampling of the principal subtitles:

1. Approaches to Islam: several hadith on the Islamic state and the reestablishment of the caliphate.
2. Reply to those who are in despair.
3. The place (*dār*) where we live: *dār al-islām* versus *dār al-ḥarb*, the territory of Islam versus the territory of war.
4. The leader who governs by laws other than the revealed law.
5. Muslim leaders today are in a state of apostasy.
6. A comparison between the Mongols and today's leaders.

7. The compilations of *fatāwā* [legal opinions] by Ibn Taymiyya are useful in the present age.
8. How does one treat, according to the law, those Muslim soldiers who refuse to serve in the Mongol army?
9. Status of Mongol goods, according to Ibn Taymiyya.
10. Status of war against the Mongols.
11. Status of one who becomes a client of the Mongols against the Muslims.
12. Welfare associations.
13. Obedience, education, abundance of pious acts.
14. The foundation of a political party.
15. Straining for access to high places.
16. Nonviolent propaganda alone.
17. Emigration (Hijra).
18. Dedication to the search for knowledge (*'ilm*).
19. Why is the *umma* different from all other communities with respect to fighting on God's behalf? (Because God ordered armed jihad.)
20. The revolt against leadership.
21. The enemy within and the enemy without.
22. Reply to those who argue that jihad is only defensive.
23. The verse of the sword, Sura 9, Verse 5.
24. Society in Mecca and Medina.
25. To fight is today a duty for all Muslims.
26. Aspects of jihad are not successive phases: jihad for the soul, jihad against the devil, jihad against polytheists, jihad against hypocrites.
27. Fear of failure.
28. The nature of command (in combat).
29. The swearing of allegiance to fight until death.
30. Inciting jihad for the cause of God.
31. Punishment for failing to undertake jihad.
32. Legal quibbles and their refutation.
33. The ethical and legal rules of jihad.

Merely reading these titles enables one to identify a simple and sufficient "argument" for the mobilization of "all Muslims in despair," which is to say, all those left down and out by the nationalist struggle, by the fact of the state as employer, by economic development supported by the West, and by sociocultural uprootedness, pauperization, and marginalization. These millions of men and women have the hypothetical authority of citizens; religion lays before them the possibility of becoming persons in the image of God, but they find themselves in fact deprived of elementary rights (rights to work, housing, information, education, political participation) and of an adequate framework for religious expression. This intolerable situation renders the divine promise irrelevant, annihilates the work of the Prophet, and necessitates, as a result, recourse to combat on behalf of God—that is to say, in order to stay within the Covenant (*mīthāq*) established between God and his creatures. In this fashion, political development is interpreted with the help of the socioreligious paradigm of Medina; it calls for a solution identical to that used by the Prophet against the infidels, which Ibn Taymiyya brought up to date in Syria and used against the Mongols.

This solution is explicitly defined and prescribed by God himself in the verse of the sword.[15] Al-Faraj writes:

> Most commentators on the Qur'an have said something about a certain verse they call the Verse of the Sword (9,5). Here is that verse: "When the holy months are over, kill polytheists wherever you find them; capture them, besiege them, ambush them."
>
> Ibn Kathir noted in his exegesis of the Qur'an: Al-Dahhak ibn Muzahim said, "[This verse] annuls any treaty between the Prophet—blessing and salvation be upon him—and any infidel, along with any contract or any accord." Al-'Ufi said about this verse, according to Ibn 'Abbas: "No contract, no defense pact with an infidel was recognized after this dissolution of obligations fixed by treaty was revealed."
>
> The exegete Muh-ibn Ahmad ibn Juzayy al-Kalbi said: "The abrogation of the order to be at peace with the infidels, to pardon them, to be passively in contact with them, and to endure their insults came before the order to fight them. That makes it superfluous to repeat the abrogation of the order to live at peace with the infidels in every passage of the Qur'an. This order to live in peace with them is given in 114 verses spread among 54 suras. All of those references are abrogated by verses 9,5 and 2,216 (you are prescribed to fight)."

The text continues with other citations of authorities recognized by the "orthodox" tradition.[16] We should notice first of all the place given to citations. The Qur'an, the hadith, the teachings of authors such as Ibn Taymiyya, often called "the Teacher of Islam," and Ibn Kathir, another Hanbali authority, take up most of the manifesto. Muslims who are familiar enough with these classic texts to consult them directly tend to minimize the importance of the manifesto, invoking the modern prejudice against citation. In fact, the persuasive and mobilizational power of Islamic discourse is all the more effective when texts that are sacred or rendered sacred by the consensus of the faithful (as in the case of Ibn Taymiyya) are reactivated and readapted to social and political circumstances experienced by the great majority of people. Inside Islamic thought, citation may be discussed for its semantic pertinence, its relationship to context, and the theological legitimacy of its appeal to the Qur'an or the hadith. Furthermore, different uses of citations followed from different schools and from different hermeneutic methods in the classical epoch. The *political consensus* achieved among Islamist movements beginning in the 1970s tends to make one forget the theological issues and the historiographical debates that classical thinkers took to be critical. There is then epistemological displacement within the cognitive system unique to Islamic thought: The principle of return to founding texts is maintained, even rigidified, but the semantic and discursive manipulation of the texts is entirely subordinate to ideological ends to the exclusion of all "scientific" procedures (syntax, semantics, rhetoric, history, theology, even philosophy) that every legal expert (imam mujtahid) was supposed to master.

According to this perspective, the notion of authoring a text loses all its meaning and pertinence. Muhammad 'Abd al-Salam Faraj is only the echo of a collective voice; his manifesto represents a social imaginary hanging on all the connotations, politico-religious resonances, and raised hopes that it introduces. Thousands of mosque sermons, public harangues, articles, conferences, and published works carry and distribute broadly the same emotional charge using the same citations and the same vocabulary, and their effectiveness is all the greater because they are constantly reutilized in ritual fashion. Like a swollen river picking up a wild assortment of things in its path, the rich Islamic tradition of protest in the name of the absolute Truth revealed by God is called upon to play the same revolutionary role as in its first manifestation in Mecca and Medina. The jihad was, in fact, the military response of the Prophet to the threats of destruction that "polytheists" and "infidels"—polemical designations elevated by the Qur'an to religious categories set apart for eternity—brought to bear on the "believers," the "faithful," that is, the Muslim minority group then emerging as a new social, political, and cultural force. The Qur'an reproached unbelieving bedouins (uncooperative with the new cause), who refused to participate in jihad, with the same vehemence and "spiritual" indignation expressed by the collective voice represented by the manifesto.

In this manner, the Medina experience introduced a paradigm of historical action with the help of discourse that mixed spiritual élan with the need for political struggle and functioned as a *founding tale*[17] for the believing community.

One can distinguish the following traits in the cognitive system underlying the whole of the manifesto and the whole of the collective text of which the manifesto is but a fragment:

1. Everything happens within a dogmatic closure marked off by the Qur'anic corpus and the semantic and legal-theological extensions that "orthodox" tradition has selected, consecrated, and transmitted.

2. Attention focuses on divine commandment and the obligation of each believer to obey.

3. The norm established to guide practical conduct in the society of believers takes priority and primacy to the point of nullifying 114 verses, which nonetheless represented God's teaching spread over several years of apostleship.

4. The crucial issue of abrogation is definitively settled by those "authorities" consecrated by the tradition; in fact, there was debate among classical ulema about principle and modalities.

5. Polytheists, infidels, and the faithful are no longer considered as competing social groups but as theological-juridical categories enjoying the same legal qualities in very different historical contexts.

6. Historical and sociological contingencies that provoked the commandments contained in Sura 9, Verse 5, and Sura 2, Verse 216, are sublimated and

transcendentalized as a result of the general framework of signification established by the phenomenon of revelation.

7. The authorities consecrated by the tradition participate fully and authentically
in the phenomenon of revelation: Their information is beyond dispute, their
interpretations infallible; they constitute so many dogmatic landmarks and
serve as guarantors of the "logical," "coherent" functioning of Islamic discourse.

The seven traits I have just distinguished are also postulates constituting the epistemological armor of Islamic discourse as it functioned from the moment the Qur'an
was established as a Closed Official Corpus (*mushaf*) of revealed enunciations and
read as such by the authorized experts. Semantic extensions, even explosions, are unlimited and recurrent, as the manifesto proves, but the strategies of orthodox interpretation engendered more or less narrow dogmatic closure according to the cognitive (i.e., philosophical, theological, or mystical) and/or ideological (legal, militant)
questions addressed to the Qur'an as a whole. The "Muslim" person develops and asserts himself or herself within dogmatic closure, portrayed as the only, irreplaceable
domain of orthodox "truth" within the whole domain of the Muslim *thinkable,* as
opposed to the *unthinkable,* to which no one can accede without violating the
boundaries of dogmatic closure.

The long citations of text from Ibn Taymiyya in the manifesto confirm all the
characteristic traits of the Islamic cognitive system. The authors use an authority of
the fourteenth century both to go back to the Medina experience and to certify the
transhistoric validity of Islamic protest, still suitable for the twentieth century,
against the disorders of the political community run by infidels. Sadat, the shah, and
Tamerlane are only so many incarnations of Pharaoh, oppressive leaders who put
profane laws in the place of legal policy (*siyāsa shar'iyya*) taught by the Qur'an, applied by the Prophet, and explained and re-evoked regularly by reformist ulema.

The historian and the sociologist must call attention to the anachronism inherent
in this approach and its nullification of the historicity of meaning as subject to the
political, economic, and cultural metamorphoses of society. In fact, we must see the
rupture between the cognitive system appropriate to societies of the Book and the
one promoted by our secularized industrial societies, homogenized by technology.
Narrative history and descriptive sociology must yield the floor to social and cultural
anthropology: The Muslim cognitive system is essentially mythical; it would thus be
wrong to judge it or to portray it only from the perspective of historical knowledge
based on reason, much less on positivism or historiography, as do many Muslim and
Western historians.

What is at stake in this theoretical approach is the exact status of the person in
societies of the Book. The access to this status depends, indeed, on the principle for
legitimation of authority upheld in these societies. Legitimation is acquired only by
appeal to the pious ancestors (*al-salaf al-ṣāliḥ*) of the inaugural age in the community
promised salvation (*al-firqa al-nājiya*). Not every individual is a person, and persons

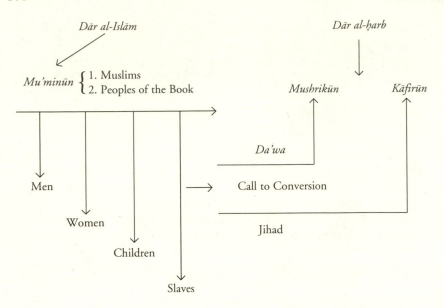

FIGURE 21.1 The longer the arrow, the greater the inferiority of status. Peoples of the Book are believers; they reflect the same hierarchy but are subject to their own jurisdictions.

are more eminent (*afḍal*) insofar as they approach the ideal of piety called for by the Qur'an and the family of the Prophet (*ashrāf*).

This general principle for the classification of persons and individuals is complicated by legal definitions of the status of men, women, children, and slaves (up until the abolition of slavery). The manifesto for the reinstitution of jihad in the current phase of history aims to halt modern developments, which tend to confuse the individual with the person by prescribing the secular notion of citizen, one who enjoys equal rights to exercise functions and to play roles open to everyone in the society. The sharp controversy about the status of women in Muslim societies results from the collision of the traditional model (reinstitution of revealed law) with the modern declaration of human rights.

The perspective of the manifesto is also that of the Crusades and other wars of religion. It is the perspective of "societies of the Book." War must be directed against infidels, nonpersons who inhabit the zone of war (*dār al-ḥarb*). Each of the societies of the Book thus expresses the hierarchical vision illustrated in Figure 21.1.

Faced with this vision "legitimating" yesterday's tragedies as well as today's, how can religion escape dogmatic closure? The West followed the path of secularism, which attenuated tensions between religious and political authorities and assigned matters such as economics, justice, and scientific research to autonomous spheres of activity; however, the West has still not succeeded in responding to growing demands for moral and spiritual values grounded in scientific truth. In other words, the problem of the person is still unresolved despite long-standing political and scientific practices based on the postulate of the inevitable withering away of religion. Durkheim eloquently expressed this "scientific" conviction in these terms:

> In the beginning, [religion] extends to everything; everything that is social is religious; the two words are synonymous. Then, little by little, political, economic, and scientific functions free themselves from the religious function, establish themselves separately, and take on a more and more temporal character. If one may express it this way, God, who was first present in all human relations, pulls out progressively, leaving the world to men and their conflicts. Or, if he continues to control them, he does so from on high and from afar.[18]

Before examining how current scientific thought tries to go beyond this reductionist theory of religion, I must emphasize that Islamic thought, still imprisoned in dogmatic closure, is not yet familiar with the educational experiments and pragmatic solutions carried out in Western societies ever since the eighteenth century. This realm is what I have called the "unthought" in Islamic thought. What is needed is a comparison of Islamic thought with scientific thought that all the while guards against scientism.

It goes without saying that Islamic thought as it is practiced in ordinary Islamic discourse rejects without examination the very principle of such a comparison. The strategy of refusal is well known in every dogmatic cognitive system. There is, however, a legitimate aspect of this refusal. Insofar as scientific thought recognized by the community of scholars is linked to historical experience and Western languages, one must be careful not to repeat the error of Aristotelianism in elevating distinctions made by the First Teacher in the Greek language into universal categories.

Moreover, what is at stake in the comparison, now as before, is the ultimate foundation of values that establish the person and shape his or her thought and action. Traditional religions located this foundation and succeeded in rooting it in the beliefs of everyone. Scientific thought has corralled the expressions and carriers testifying to the mental existence of this foundation: "gesture, world, text, building, institution, person, group."[19] But it has failed to objectify the nature of the religious.

This does not mean that we must give in to the current wave of religiosity, which serves as a spiritualist veil for psychological and political demands clearly linked to structural upheaval in our societies. I discern two possible lines of complementary research for getting beyond reductionist theory, dogmatic refusal, and spiritualist speculation about the "values" and principles of legitimation. Religious anthropology must integrate the three revealed religions into its research, ending its exclusion of the Islamic example, and Islamic thought must get out of its dogmatic closure to benefit from the tools and questioning of the social sciences, *enriched* by the problematic of societies of the Book.

Western scholars are both fascinated by Islam and repulsed by it. They want very much to listen to what Muslims say about themselves, their religion, and their societies, but they decline to use the Islamic example as a starting point for reflections on religion as a phenomenon. Although the beneficiary of a very stimulating scientific environment, Christianity remains outside new movements of thought; one can thus imagine how much Islam, a fortiori, is still riveted to the collective representations of the impoverished masses. There is a sort of consensus, among anthropologists in particular, that it is best to stay away from the domain of revealed religions and to devote energy instead to the study of the old tribal societies of Africa, Australia, Oceania, and America.[20] Must we explain this "prudence" by the fact that scholars belong to religions that continue to play essential roles in their own societies? Judaism, Christianity, and Islam are on a par in this regard.

Is it dereliction, prudence, or indifference on the part of scholars? As far as Islam is concerned, we must also consider the professional strategy of many scholars: They don't push analysis in directions that would lead to the abolition of taboos accumulated by official Islam ever since nationalist states first sketched the limits of permissible exploration. Thus the scientific community, although free in theory to tackle any subject and to reveal the mechanisms of control utilized in any organized form of social life, prefers to engage in ideological complicity with dominant groups. What is more, certain renowned Orientalists have helped to enrich the apologetic literature on Islam.

Research on Islam as a religion is blocked because Muslims more and more suffer under political, cultural, and psychological constraints that are reinforced in their own societies, while Islamicists fascinated with the political efficacy of "fundamentalists" give priority to a short-term perspective and to politically oriented descriptions of events rather than taking the long view and joining the indispensable critique of the Islamic cognitive system in its epistemic armament.

Recognizing this neglect, I have tried to show[21] that the phenomenon of revelation is not a problem reserved for theologians. Revelation is a point of strategic intervention for the historian of Qur'anic text and exegetic literature; for the linguist-semiotician interested in the theory of religious discourse and the critique of theological discourse; for the sociologist concerned with belief, hope, religious discourse, and religious practice tied to the Qur'an and/or to archaic local traditions; for the psychologist studying the internalization of "values" and of symbolic religious capital and the role of "revelation" in the psycho- and sociocultural integration of the person; for the jurist interested in the origins and foundations of the so-called religious law; and for the anthropologist looking at revelation as a discourse legitimating all sorts of domination—political, economic, psychological, and symbolic: of man over woman, adult over infant and adolescent, employer over worker, leader over subject-citizen, saint over faithful, spiritual teacher over aspiring disciple, learned clerk (*'ālim*) over layman.

All these hierarchies still function and maintain the validity of the cognitive system founded on the primacy of revelation. By looking more closely, one can reconstruct all the sociocultural mechanisms underpinning the social order and the "legitimacy" of the political order, which in turn tightly condition the status and development of the person.

One could no doubt search out these problems and treat them within current topics such as the state, civil society, authority and power, myth and historicity, systems of production and exchange, elementary kinship structures, and the sociology of law. Western scientific practice is much more comfortable when it puts off, avoids, or gets rid of the religious question. That is why there are essays about Islam devoted to the different topics I have just enumerated. But such essays are very often limited in scientific ambition, information, practical and theoretical support, and especially in number. How can one justify scientifically the setting aside, the methodological suspension, or the explicit elimination from consideration of the religious element in societies where, contrary to what Durkheim said at the beginning of the century, God is present at every level of social existence and every level of discourse expressing it? Might we not consider the idea that scientific thought can and should utilize the societies of the Book as examples of religion opening itself to learned, rationalized culture and all the while perpetuating symbolic practices that transform mental realities into a constraining social order?

Contemporary Muslim societies are, in this respect, laboratories rich in what they can teach the social sciences. But they remain underanalyzed and very badly understood because the places for training scholars are insufficient or inappropriate and because the available methods and conceptual equipment are inadequate to decipher situations, practices, beliefs, institutions, and what are often unique patterns of development. I am thinking, for example, of sexuality, kinship structures, legal codes combining traditional Muslim and modern law, confrontations between codes of honor and the imperatives of an industrial economy, contradictions between the law-based state and the patrimonial state, tensions and gaps between the utopian vision of authority and the exercise of oppressive authority.

The cultural, intellectual, and spiritual patrimony accumulated in the Islamic tradition has always nourished the aspiration for the ideal person, the perfect human being, *al-insān al-kāmil.* God established the characteristics and the paths toward realization. Saints, mystics, and thinkers drew up the itinerary both in their personal lives and in the reports of their experience they left behind. A powerful nostalgia for being, inseparable from the "*dur désir de durer*" (the determination to live on) that grips every mind coming into contact with the promise of eternal life, sustains every Muslim just as it does Jewish and Christian believers, nourished by the promises of the Holy Scriptures. This irreducible fact about human beings from societies of the Book seeks expression and reincarnation in the multiple forms and types of existence proffered by modernity. Scientific thought tends to diminish this constitutive element of the person rather than to integrate it into an effort to enhance human beings by means other than the rationalized imaginary, which all too often replaces the mythical imaginary.

Notes

1. N. Berdiaev, *Cinq méditations sur l'existence* (Paris: Aubier, 1936), p. 180.

2. Marcel Mauss deserves credit for elaborating in 1938 a concept of the person as a "category of the human mind." Some interesting extensions of this initial effort can be found in a recent book by M. Carrithers, S. Collins, and L. Lukes, *The Category of the Person: Anthropology, Philosophy, History* (Cambridge: Cambridge University Press, 1985). In the philosophical vein, Christian thinkers have been especially drawn to the theme and idea. See Ivan Gobry, *La personne*, 3rd ed. (Paris: PUF, 1985), for a precise explanation of this idea.

3. Mohammed Arkoun, "Emergences et problèmes dans le monde musulman contemporain (1960–1985)," *Islamochristiania*, no. 12 (1986), pp. 135–161.

4. I would cite the works of Pierre Bourdieu for Kabylia, *Le sens pratique* (Paris: Editions de Minuit, 1980); the recent work of Lila Abu-Lughod, *Veiled Sentiments: Honor and Poetry in a Bedouin Society* (Berkeley: University of California, 1986); and Germaine Tillion, *Le harem et les cousins* (Paris: Editions du Seuil, 1966).

5. Abu-Lughod, *Veiled Sentiments*, p. 233.

6. Abram Kardiner, *L'individu dans la société* (Paris: Gallimard, 1969).

7. In two essays, one dedicated to al-Ghazali, the other to the emergence of leaders in the contemporary Muslim world, I have already sketched a move in this direction. See "Révélations, vérité et histoire dans l'oeuvre de Ghazâlì," in *Essais sur la pensée islamique,* 3rd ed. (Paris: Maisonneuve et Larose, 1984); "Imaginaire social et leaders dans le monde musulman contemporain," in *Arabica* (1988), pp. 18–35. For a more developed anthropological problematic see M. Godelier, *La production des grands hommes* (Paris: Fayard, 1982).

8. Tafkir Wal-Hijra is another spinoff, like al-Jihad, from the Muslim Brotherhood in Egypt.

9. Marcel Gaucher, *La désenchantement du monde* (Paris: Gallimard, 1982).

10. See my *Lectures du Coran* (Paris: Maisonneuve et Larose, 1982).

11. Gilles Kepel, *Muslim Extremism in Egypt: The Prophet and the Pharaoh,* translated by Jon Rothschild (Berkeley: University of California, 1986).

12. Johannes J.G. Jansen, *The Neglected Duty: The Creed of Sadat's Assassins and Islamic Resurgence in the Middle East* (New York: Macmillan, 1986), p. xvii. The italics are mine.

13. *Radical Islam* is the title of Emmanuel Sivan's book (New Haven: Yale, 1985).

14. I urge readers to refer to the Arabic version, if possible, to pick up the system of connotations within the Islamic logosphere.

15. I have written a long analysis of this verse, "Les sciences de l'homme et de la société appliquées à l'étude de l'islam," *Les sciences sociales in Algérie* (Alger: OPU, 1986).

16. I have sketched a definition of this system of thought in "L'islam dans l'histoire," *Maghreb-Machreq,* no. 102 (1983).

17. There are many examples of founding tales in ancient epics, in the Bible, and in the Qur'an.

18. Emile Durkheim, *De la division du travail social,* 4th ed. (Paris: Alcan, 1922), pp. 143–144.

19. Emile Poulat, "Epistémologie," in Marc Guillaume, *L'état des sciences sociales en France* (Paris: La Découverte, 1986), p. 400.

20. As testified by the work of Claude Lévi-Strauss in *La notion de la personne en Afrique noire,* edited by G. Dieterlen (Paris: CNRS, 1973). Anthropological bibliographies on Muslim

societies comfirm the distinction I have already made between narrative history, descriptive sociology, and classic Islamology, on one hand, and ethnography, ethnology, and anthropology still free of ethnographism, on the other.

21. Mohammed Arkoun, *The Concept of Revelation: From Ahl al-Kitāb to the Societies of the Book,* Occasional Papers, Claremont Graduate School, 1988.

❧ 22 ❧

Human Rights

Who is the audience for an "Islamic" discourse on human rights? What rela-
tionship can be established between what we call Islam with a capital "I" and
nation-states founded for the most part after World War II? Still more gener-
ally, what meaning can be assigned to the idea of an exclusively divine origin of
human rights? What is one to make of the "philosophical" or "secular" assertion
that human beings win their rights by sociopolitical struggle and cultural pro-
gress—without external help? In what philosophical direction can we or should
we orient research on the foundations of human rights and the means of assur-
ing their implementation?

Like Jews and Christians, contemporary Muslims have shown concern for human
rights, but they have attempted to demonstrate that the original matrix for a culture
based on human rights comes from the Qur'an and the teaching of the Prophet
Muhammad. This drive to reclaim for Islam a vision of human beings and a practice
of law and politics that, in fact, only gained credence with the English, American,
and especially the French revolutions was clearly demonstrated at a UNESCO meet-
ing of September 19, 1981, where a Universal Islamic Declaration of Human Rights
was prepared on the initiative of the Islamic Council and its secretary general, Salem
Azzam. In the West there has always been a tendency to exclude Islam from the cultural domain where human rights were conceived and proclaimed and where they retain meaning. The Universal Islamic Declaration of Human Rights was a response to
that exclusion. "Eminent scholars, Muslim jurists, and representatives of movements
and currents of Islamic thought" prepared the text of this declaration, and all twenty-
three articles are based on verses of the Qur'an or on selections from official Sunni
compilations of hadith. No reference is made to the canonic corpus of Shi'i hadith.

The principles asserted in the introduction permit us to identify the theological
postulates dictating the very notion of rights:

> Islam gave humanity an ideal code of human rights 1400 years ago. The purpose of
> these rights is to confer honor and dignity on humanity and to eliminate exploitation,
> oppression, and injustice. Human rights in Islam are deeply rooted in the conviction
> that God, and God alone, is the author of Law and the source of all human rights.
> Given this divine origin, no leader, no government, no assembly or any other author-
> ity can restrict, abrogate or violate in any manner the rights conferred by God.

The great virtue of this declaration is that it expresses the convictions, modes of thought, and demands that contemporary Muslims are coming to embrace. Historians may decry the anachronism of projecting modern concepts backward toward the founding age, the mythical age of Islam; the jurist may emphasize the ethical idealism of articles that are dead letters and even openly violated in all Muslim countries. Such exercises are only too easy, but one could also apply them to a variety of statements made in the West since the American Declaration of Independence of 1776 (a philosophical exposition of human rights by Thomas Jefferson) and the more elaborate declaration of 1789 in France. History continues to represent suffering for a majority of human beings, and even in countries that have already struggled hard for human rights, such as France, examples of shortcomings and backwardness continue to surface. Moreover, to cloak such precious rights as religious freedom, freedom of association, freedom of thought, and freedom of travel in the full authority of the Islamic tradition is not a negligible accomplishment.

The questions posed at the beginning of this chapter do not arise in the context of intelligibility invoked by the authors of the Islamic Declaration. The divine origin of all creation cannot be the object of questioning, and legislation is for God alone. In a militantly secular context, the religious origin of human rights does not constitute a pertinent question, either; if evoked at all, it serves to emphasize a revolutionary break that, in the view of reductionist positivists, rescues human beings from "alienation."

A critical reexamination and reworking of the concept of Truth-Right (*al-ḥaqq*) and of its foundations are both possible and necessary. Let's keep in mind that the Qur'anic term *al-ḥaqq* applies to God himself as well as to absolute, transcendent Truth, sender and receiver of the "rights of God" (*ḥuqūq allah*). By respecting these rights one puts oneself in the right, *al-ḥaqq*, sees the true reality, and benefits from the rights that follow from it. In the Arabic language, the movement from the singular *ḥaqq* to the plural *ḥuqūq* translates a desacralization of right extracted from the religious force of *al-ḥaqq* and dispersed in the management of contingent, profane, individual rights. Analysis must proceed in two directions:

1. The apologetic function and inspiration of the text are undeniable. It is a matter of showing not only that Islam as a religion is open to the proclamation and defense of human rights but also that the Qur'an, the Word of God, defined these rights at the beginning of the seventh century, well before Western revolutions. The desire for and process of recuperation employed by contemporary Judaism and Christianity translate the same apologetic tendency. Although this practice quite rightly shocks the historian, one must not lose sight of the current utility of finding authorities within the religious tradition to consecrate rights that need to be taught and defended in the oppressive political contexts unfortunately so widespread in today's world.

2. The critical and historical reexamination of the actual contents of the Holy Scriptures, on the one hand, and of the modern culture of human rights, on the other, is still an urgent and indispensable intellectual task. It offers an excellent op-

portunity to shore up religious thought in general by forcing it to recognize that the highest religious teachings and revelation itself in the three monotheistic religions are subject to *historicity.*

The ideological conditions and the cultural limits that distinguished the birth and development of human rights in the West must be the object of the same sort of critical reexamination to illuminate the weaknesses not only in the traditional religious imaginary but in the imaginary of civil religion secreted by Western secular revolutions. It is time to open a new field of intelligibility and go beyond the mimetic competition, essentially ideological, between traditional religions and civil religion, itself bound to the powerful phenomenon described by Fernand Braudel under the title of material civilization.

Islamic thought has always included a discourse on the rights of God and the rights of man (*ḥuqūq allah/ḥuqūq adam*), with the former having primacy and priority over the latter. That is why traditional thought insists that each believer perform the five canonical obligations: profession of faith (*shahāda*), prayer, almsgiving, fasting at Ramadan, and the pilgrimage to Mecca. It is through obedience that the faithful internalize the notion of the rights of God; summoned to obey in this way, all creatures find themselves constrained to respect the social and political conditions for living completely this relationship between rights of God and rights of man. In other words, the respect of human rights is an aspect of, and a basic condition for, respecting the rights of God.

However, the rights thus defined within the fundamental Pact (*'ahd*) or Covenant (*mīthāq*) between creature and Creator concern first the believers who form a spiritual community (*umma*). Potentially these rights touch all human beings and are universal insofar as all human beings are called upon to enter the Covenant. In the real world, theological categories have conveyed different legal statuses. The great schism creating a simple dichotomy between faithful and infidel gave way to complication and several types of status:

1. Inside the *umma,* a great split (*al-fitna-l-kubrā*) produced competing communities: Sunni, Shi'a, and Khariji, each with its claim to a monopoly of *ḥaqq,* of the Truth-Right that governed the members of the ideal orthodox community in their earthly relations and in their relationship with God.

2. Beyond believers, there were peoples of the Book (*ahl al-kitāb*) who enjoyed a status (*dhimmī*) protected by the Islamic government. Polytheists (*mushrikūn*) lived outside the guarantees offered by the Divine Law. In legal terms there was thus a clear demarcation between the living space of Islam (*dār al-islām*), where the Divine Law (*shari'a*) was applied, and the land of war (*dār al-ḥarb*), where the Divine Law could potentially be applied some day.

3. Inside the orthodox *umma* itself, there were obviously important differences among free men, slaves, women, and children. Those distinctions are found in other legal systems and linked to the general development of law and the transition from traditional systems of law, all more or less influenced by dogmatic theologies, to modern positive law.

What we call "modernity" made a brutal eruption into the "living space of Islam" with the intrusion of colonialism as a historical fact. Seen strictly in terms of the development and diffusion of human rights in the framework of intellectual modernity, the colonial fact poses problems for both the West and Muslim countries. We must pause here to untangle what is a very confused ideological situation for both sides.

Colonial endeavors of nineteenth-century Europe sought justification in what was called a civilizing mission. It was a matter of raising "backward" peoples to the level of a "universal" culture and civilization. According to this perspective, for colonizing countries such as France, human rights appeared to be exported along with modern culture and civilization. The Catholic and Protestant churches participated in this movement by implanting missionary outposts even in the land of Islam.

The colonial adventure ended badly. It is difficult to speak to a Muslim audience today about the Western origin of human rights without provoking indignant protests. We must not lose sight of the wars of liberation and the ongoing, postcolonial battle against Western "imperialism" if we want to understand the psychological and ideological climate in which an Islamic discourse on human rights has developed in the past ten or fifteen years.

The development of that discourse is without doubt based on mimetic overbidding; it picks up the enunciations of Western declarations and confers upon them an Islamic origin. The operation, essentially ideological, conceals a crucial difference: A powerful movement of Enlightenment philosophy had already prepared the way for a declaration of human rights in eighteenth-century England, America, and France. Moreover, the rise of the bourgeoisie to rival the nobility and clergy created a social and economic force capable of insuring that political application of the new ideas of equality, liberty, and fraternity would at least begin.

In the nineteenth century, Muslim countries encountered only fragments, or heard only faint echoes, of the philosophical Enlightenment. A very small number of intellectuals, scholars, journalists, politicians, and travelers had access to the schools, universities, and literatures of the West. It was the so-called liberal epoch. Arab, Indian, Indonesian, Turkish, and Iranian elites believed they could cause their countries to benefit from the light cast by science and the political revolutions of Europe. Even the reformist movement known as *salafī* ("orthodox") initiated by Jamal al-Din al-Afghani and then continued by Muhammad 'Abdu, showed itself hospitable to the philosophy of human freedom that inspired the discourse on human rights. Nationalist leaders such as Farhat Abbas (Algeria), Habib Bourguiba (Tunisia), Allal al-Fassi (Morocco), Michel Aflaq (Syria), and even Gamal abdel Nasser (Egypt), as well as the first leaders of the Algerian war of liberation, referred to the great principles of 1789. As for Turkey, Atatürk, with excessive zeal, imposed a secular revolution on a country of long-standing Islamic tradition.

The intellectual and political elites of the Muslim world, unlike those in France and England, could not find support in a rather enlightened and dynamic social class capable of animating secular institutions and of creating a state apparatus corresponding to the new ideas. In the new states linked to the Islamic tradition, much more than in the countries where such conceptions were born, human rights based in Enlightenment philosophy remain a set of idealistic demands and a theme for the anticolonial struggle, but they lack cultural and social rootedness.

Classical Islam (seventh to the thirteenth centuries) had lost its dynamism and its capacity for self-renewal long before the advent of colonialism in all these countries. With the triumph of the ideology of national liberation in the 1950s, a great historical confusion beset many minds: The breach with the civilization of classical Islam was attributed exclusively to colonial intrusion and then in turn to the "imperial" domination that took its place after the reconquest of political sovereignties. The discourse of the so-called Islamic revolution in Iran took up the great themes of the ideology of national liberation, which retained a socialist, secular coloration, and reworked them to include Islamic sources and to encompass struggle against Westernization.

The new states all developed a political willfulness that nationalized religion along with education, information, and other sectors of social life. Supervision of religion by a minister of religious affairs became necessary as a result of increasing pressure from two sides:

1. Demography amplified social and economic demands. It conferred upon Islam a primordial role in structuring, channeling, and inaugurating a discourse of demands, which were not tolerated in direct political form.
2. Unable to legitimate its authority by democratic procedures, the state resorted to Islam to legitimate its presence and its policy of modernization, all the while keeping open a line of communication to the masses. In this way, the necessary recourse to material civilization and technology as bearers of modernity could be reconciled with inevitable traditionalization through a return to the Islamic model of legislation, government, and culture.

The reconciliation was above all a do-it-yourself ideology. It suggested submitting societies to all the processes of economic development imported from the West while reestablishing or reinforcing the cultural *signals* of Islamic identity: construction of mosques, encouragement of religious education, foundation of Islamic universities or theological schools, wearing of traditional dress, and the application of the *shari'a*.

Where jurists tried, as in Algeria, to form a league for human rights to protect citizens, the state itself felt under attack and retaliated by refusing to grant permission to organize and prosecuting the instigators. It solicited the formation of a competing association to seize the initiative in this domain without threatening the establishment. At that moment the Islamic Declaration of Human Rights acquired its ideological and psychological purpose: to reassure, in effect, believer-citizens by proclaiming that God guaranteed rights, to undercut secular demands of Western origin, and to reestablish confidence in the "modernity" of Islamic law and its universal and intangible character.

There is a profound and indestructible conspiracy between states in search of legitimacy; the collective conscience eager for justice, civil liberties, and political par-

ticipation; and nations aroused by an old, mythic desire for unity. (The eschatological expectation of the spiritual *umma* converges with the political hopes for national
unity according to the Western, nationalist model of the nineteenth century.) I see
Islamic difficulties with human rights within a specific set of historical circumstances
and social, complexities. Therefore, I appreciate the pertinence of research on the
meaning of the opposition between divine and secular origins of human rights.

The question about human rights is first historical, then philosophical. Its heightened importance in our time reflects the return to religion and lack of intellectual
and cultural preparation to discuss the question in all its dimensions: historic rupture
with the conditions for the emergence of human rights in different cultures; development of the very notion of right; political decisions on the separation of spheres of
human existence—temporal and spiritual, secular and religious; "scientific" judgments about the intelligence of the totality called "world" and our place in it; extension of so-called "rational" political groupings, which are in fact highly ideological.

Language is a social link, an irreducible force prescribed for all. For Muslim
societies, language remains impregnated with "values" and religious references,
whereas in the West, so-called scientific rationality and the therapeutic, even messianic, virtue of human rights discourse in a secular, desacralized context have replaced
religious language. In both cases, critical reevaluations and new types of intelligibility
are indispensable to show that, even in modern secularized culture cut off from the
divine, human rights presuppose the sacredness of human beings. I am not speaking
of the traditional notion of the sacred proclaimed by contemporary Islamic discourse
but utterly violated in the most widespread of political, social, and economic practices; I am not speaking either of an artificial resacralization in the style of the cult of
the Supreme Being installed by the French Revolution. The sacredness of human beings must result from a cultivation and an even broader and richer implementation of
human rights.

To think simultaneously in an Islamic context about the positive contributions of
secularism and the enduring values of religion is surely possible, but only for the very
long term. Current political and sociological circumstances militate against that enterprise. Modes of intelligibility in classical Islamic thought are much too tied to medieval mental space to permit a correct interpretation and an integration of modernity. The models put to work by Western thought are themselves either inadequate
or perceived as a strategy of cultural domination from which Muslims must protect
themselves. This situation fully justifies the question posed at the outset: In what
philosophical direction can we or should we orient research on the foundations of
human rights and the means of assuring their implementation?

Current Islamic thought believes it can confront and defy the thought and historical experience of the West where the philosophical foundations of human rights
have been progressively eroded. To proclaim human rights, or even to guarantee
them on a strictly legal level, is not enough if the human calling to transcend the human condition and human achievement is not founded on undebatable, universal,
transhistoric teachings. Islam, like the Christianity of the early Church Fathers, in-

sists on the spiritual calling of human beings. Created in the image of God, human beings are summoned to join God in eternal life. Muslim law first defines the rights of God (*ḥuqūq allah*); the legal manuals begin by treating rules for the fulfillment of canonical obligations (*'ibādāt*) before passing to a discussion of worldly transactions (*mu'amalāt*). Thus, all rights accorded to others in business transactions and other civil matters are linked to the rights of God, which impart value as well as sacred and ontological guarantees.

The methodology of Muslim law (*uṣūl al-fiqh*) defines intellectual and "scientific" procedures that prescribe a religious way of perceiving the whole of the law elaborated by the jurists. That theoretical structure permits law to be sacralized by locating its roots (*taṣīl*) in sacred texts: the Qur'an and the prophetic traditions (*uṣūl*). In effect, the faithful still perceive religious law (*shari'a*) as a Divine Law rooted in revelation. That is why people demand a political regime that protects and applies this law and rejects all legislation of human origin.

The rights enumerated in the American Declaration of Independence remain linked to their religious origins. The English and French revolutions took more decisive steps toward secular philosophical foundations without completely breaking away from a rationalizing spirituality. The massive return to religious affirmation, even in the West, forces me to pose or repose the problem of revelation in the three monotheistic religions, no longer starting with traditional theological definitions but with the data and requirements of a modern hermeneutic. We can think about human rights in a secular framework today only if we can intellectually and culturally get a hold on all the problems, old and new, linked to the phenomenon of revelation. This work has not yet been undertaken or even perceived in the terms and framework that I am suggesting here. It is indeed a fact that the streams of theological discourse coming from the three communities continue to function as strategies of self-justification and thus of reciprocal exclusion aimed at preserving a monopoly on control of revelation and of all the symbolic capital that flows from it. The prevalent attitudes of these religious traditions toward the origins of human rights illustrate perfectly these self-serving tendencies. Historical criticism is too often missing; all seek in particular to annex for themselves the ethical-legal privileges and the ideological functions that now more than ever are attached to the bewitching theme of human rights. I have tried hard to keep from falling into this error myself.

To approach the question of how to insure implementation of human rights in contemporary Muslim societies, one can work from the constitutions adopted by various regimes. By integrating the principle of respect for human rights, a large number of states have created a legal arena where it is theoretically possible for citizens to respond to violations by initiating protest procedures. Here as elsewhere, reality differs greatly from principle, but creating a legal arsenal for potential future use is not a negligible achievement. With the exception of Turkey, launched by Atatürk into a radical, secular experiment, the first constituent assemblies in the Muslim countries all tried to reconcile Islam and modern legislation. One would have to analyze each case to be able to assess the differences, the bold steps, the successes, the delays, and the breaches with Islam and continuity.

These developments are far from complete. The Islamist movements have brought about an ideological hardening that rejects modernity and restores elements of the *shari'a*—utterly out of context and juxtaposed with legal codes borrowed from the West. The status of women suffers most, especially from legislation where intent diverges widely from effect. That is why questions about human rights cannot be posed in the same way for women as for men. A set of provisions called the "personal statute" (*al-aḥwāl al-shakhsiyya*) continues to govern the condition of women in many countries. To touch that would generate theological problems heretofore ill- or unformulated. Above and beyond theological objections, the philosophical status of the person is at stake.

Much remains to be done in all societies so that "human rights" are not mere words designed to assuage the thirst for liberty, justice, dignity, and equality all human beings experience. Religions have performed significant educative and therapeutic functions over the centuries, but their effectiveness has always been limited either by misuse at the hands of clerics or by weaknesses inherent in traditional cultural systems. One cannot, indeed, judge the effect of religious teachings on the emancipation of the human condition without evaluating the cultures that have refined, diffused, and applied those teachings.

Religion, like language, is a collective force that governs the life of societies. Secular religions have taken over for traditional religions in this regard. It is illusory and dangerous to ask of religions more than they can give. Only human beings, with their creativity and their innovative boldness, can constantly renew and augment opportunities for their own liberation.

23

Ethics and Politics

Does militant Islamic political discourse possess ethical foundations and inter-est in a political philosophy through which it could enunciate its aims and anchor its values? Does it accommodate ethical and political thought in an at-tempt to channel, nourish, and legitimate the militant actions and great procla-mations of revolutionary movements? Are there isolated intellectuals or groups of them in Muslim societies today who push toward critical and constructive re-flection in recurrent discussion on crucial points such as power and legitimacy, human rights and the emancipation of the feminine condition, application of the shari'a in the form bequeathed from the Middle Ages, ethics in economic and financial life, social justice and the distribution of national resources, the rights of children and particularly of illegitimate children (nonexistent in clas-sical Muslim law), the place of non-Muslims in the Muslim political commu-nity, the status of the person, and the ethics of international relations?

$\mathcal{T}$he vehemence with which today's Islam expresses itself politically impresses all ob-servers. They see a paradox: a religion that has insisted so much on the transcendence and oneness of God, privileging the relationship between man and the absolute, has continually acquiesced in the deviance of militant political discourse, especially since the 1970s. The contemporary militance can be traced to the rise of the Muslim Brothers in Egypt during the 1930s, but because they never held power, their dis-course maintained a religious tone. Such a tone is scarcely to be found in the various radicalizing movements of the past twenty years.

However extensive the elaboration of ethical and political theory in contemporary Islam, one must go beyond it to clarify the relationship between the morality of daily life and the severe, omnipresent control of the authoritarian one-party nation-states that appeared after independence in contemporary Muslim societies. This kind of study would require combining the sociology of ethical practice with a legal-political analysis of a state organization that monopolizes power. To follow this complex and ambitious course, one should at the outset elaborate the circumstances in which modern thinking is debated, putting theoretical knowledge in critical perspective. A reference to the critical analysis of Jürgen Habermas on the "philosophical discourse of modernity"[1] should suffice to indicate the size of the task I am targeting.

The reader may be surprised that I have chosen to take a detour through the dis-course of modernity before examining ethical and political thought in contemporary

Islam. Western Islamicists never bother with such preliminaries, which they deem useless for reporting the positions and teachings unique to Islam. They are solely interested in "concrete" manifestations and explicit pronouncements, which become objects of narrative transposition in the manner of the social sciences applied to non-Western societies. With few exceptions, Muslim Islamicists[2] are not more interested than their Western colleagues in the conditions for *validity* of any exercise of reason, because such considerations would draw them into problematics they term purely Western. In their view, the application of such considerations to the Islamic example could only lead to unacceptable results, since the conceptual apparatus and the theoretical reasoning characteristic of Islamic thought would be polluted or ignored.

It is important to distinguish the theoretical perspective of ethics, which invites reflection on the bases of moral action, from concrete moralities, which motivate individual and collective behavior. The study of ethics reveals a contrast similar to that already discussed with respect to politics. Just as the classical period (corresponding with the Middle Ages in the West) was rich in questions, investigations, and substantial works, so the current period is characterized by flight from ethical concern. This observation may seem paradoxical to those who have let themselves be impressed by what is called the "return to religion," the "resurgence of Islam," or the "awakening of Islam." Still, one must take due notice and seek to explain the evidence: Theological research and ethical reflection have practically disappeared from the Muslim intellectual domain, ever since the initiation of scholasticism and the spirit of orthodoxy replaced the fruitful confrontations (*munāẓarāt*) of the classical age. As far as ethics is concerned, there is a precise chronological benchmark at our disposition: Miskawayh, philosopher and historian of the tenth century, composed a *Treatise on Ethics* (*Tahdhīb al-akhlāq*) that raised ethics to the rank of a full-fledged discipline of philosophy, thus laying out for the Islamic world a set of reflections equivalent to that of Aristotle's *Nicomachean Ethics* in classical Greece. The treatise incorporates, moreover, the essentials of Aristotle's theory.[3]

The great themes of the treatise were in turn picked up and Islamized in the *Balance of Moral Action* (*Mīzān al-ʿamal*) of al-Ghazali, while Nasir al-din al-Tusi (d. 1273) provided a Persian version of the same work. Since then there has been no equivalent effort in the Arabic language, and even the study of the treatise of Miskawayh practically disappeared from the curriculum after Muhammad ʿAbdu wrote a commentary at Al-Azhar in Cairo at the beginning of the century. The teaching of morality as a list of virtues and vices, the traditional division between good and evil in a "religious" perspective, persists in the schools, but there is no philosophical or theological questioning of the theoretical bases for norms that continue to be reproduced empirically.

In the classical epoch, the denunciation of moral and political behavior deemed contrary to religious and philosophical teachings in literary genres as lively as prose, poetry, historiography, and geography reinforced and completed theoretical reflection. Miskawayh wrote a famous historical essay entitled, significantly, "The Experiences of Nations" (*Tajārib al-umam*). He looked at the society of his time with the eyes of a philosopher completely enamored of the theory of moral and political action.

Here is, for example, how the geographer Ibn Hawqal castigated the princes of his time, the tenth century:

> Princes care more about today than tomorrow. Forbidden pleasures and vanities of the world divert them from the prescriptions of the Most High, the duties of government, and their role as leaders. They keep a close eye on the goods of merchants and the properties of their subjects so that they can grab them by trickery, spreading their nets and their traps to catch this game. ... They have only one manifest desire, that of hearing others pray for them and utter their name in public places. It matters little to them that cities of the frontier need reinforcement from them in cattle, water reserves, soldiers, equipment, and materiel. ... Busy as they are amassing and protecting goods, they forget to do what is good for their people and to think about the misfortunes that come from them.[4]

One is struck by the great relevance of these themes to all contemporary Muslim discussion and wit—to the popular stories that flower, especially in Egypt and Algeria, for example. There is a difference, however. Ibn Hawqal, a very sophisticated geographer, could express this social and political critique from his position as a renowned intellectual. Today's intellectuals remain silent or commit themselves openly to the support of those princes who exercise power.

Another passage from Ibn Hawqal, this one about the Byzantines, makes one think irresistibly of the feeling so often expressed by Muslims with regard to Israel and Western imperialism. This lucid intellectual assessed the permanence and depth of moral and intellectual weakness in Islam:

> The Byzantines managed to impose a truce on the inhabitants, whose long-standing habits acquired in the territory of Islam had rendered them fearful. I mean that they had become habituated to discouragement, the disappearance of authority, and lack of faith. ... It could be said that the people of today are too overwhelmed to think about authority and the death of their beliefs. ... Alas, given the current state of souls and hearts, Islam plays too big a part in palaver and disorder, rebellion, dispute, and interminable internal struggles, such that the Byzantines have free rein to put their hands on that which was previously unavailable to them and to fix their desires on that which was forbidden.

It is interesting to note Ibn Hawqal's use of the word "Islam" to designate the social and historical community, that is, that which we would today call Syrian, Moroccan, or Turkish society. At the same time, the community thus designated is implicitly presented as carrier of a divine message and of moral values to raise it above its weaknesses. Intellectuals condemned these shortcomings on the basis of a political and moral ideal that penetrated the community, trained as it was in a cultural system known by the name of *adab,* or humanism.[5]

What ought we to think of the complete *breakdown* of the humanistic tradition that permitted intellectuals to play a critical role in society and about the *continuity* of weaknesses, failures, sociocultural disorder, and political absolutism—all of which seem to have structural foundations? The question is immense. Taken seriously, both scientifically and intellectually, the breakdown undercuts the vision that Muslims have of their past and their cultural heritage, or *turāth,* as many proudly say these days, as well as of their moral and political behavior, especially since the beginning of the struggle for independence in the 1950s.

In order to avoid heaping a sort of malediction upon Muslims that would weigh upon their history, I shall stick to the comparative approach. The Hegelian idea of a moral totality linked to nostalgic evocation of the Greek polis and the first Christian communities is exactly equivalent to the Muslim invocation of an unsurpassable ideal of ethical conduct as incarnated in the person of the Prophet and his companions. The hadith, which multiplied without interruption in the first three centuries of Islam, express the cluster of ethical-religious values advocated by social groups of the most diverse circumstances and projected onto the ideal, sacralizing figures of the Pious Ancients (*al-salaf al-ṣāliḥ*). The empirical character of this morality eliminates the need for any search for theoretical legitimation. The norms assert themselves in consciousness with all the more power because they are sacralized by the authority of the Prophet.

The concept of a moral totality validated entirely by divine teaching (Qur'an, hadith) continues to dominate contemporary Islamic discourse and has even assumed an unprecedented public dimension, thanks to the multiplier effect of the media. But in terms of social psychology, this ethical-ideological vision feeds a social imaginary much more than it nourishes a sort of ethical reasoning capable of careful discernment and value critique. I thus come back to what I have already said about politics: The gulf becomes ever wider between the imaginary but obsessive representation of the prophetic model and the concrete behavior of individuals subject to the interplay of more and more severe economic, social, and political constraints. Material modernity plays a devastating role. For even the most humble, it prescribes norms of consumption, costly necessities, criteria for entry into a universally desired mode of existence. It engages all the energies and strategies of conduct in a direction that is counter to traditional morality, which is based in the subsistence economy. Structural changes affect social relationships, value hierarchies, and "moral" definitions without the agents knowing what is happening because there is scarcely any sociological, psychological, or philosophical analysis to take account of these generalized processes.

A study of money-driven corruption in contemporary Muslim societies would overturn the image of the Islamic model enjoying favor in idealistic, nostalgic discourse. In such countries there is illegal dealing even in passports for the pilgrimage to Mecca. Faced with the leadenness and shortcomings of administration and the extreme remoteness of the state, citizens have recourse to a parallel system of exchanging services with compensation in either money or favors. Obtaining visas, housing, plane tickets, commercial licenses, enrollment in a school, construction materials, places in line to buy automobiles or rare machines—all the requirements of professional and daily life are subject to tough and lucrative negotiation.

The code of honor and the symbolic capital that conferred a divine, religious, disinterested meaning to all exchanges effected at all levels of social and economic life lie far in the past. The brutal eruption of material modernity (industrialization, agrarian reform, urbanization, uprooting of rural populations, new consumption needs, travel, communication, and so on) has disrupted traditional solidarities and replaced values of fidelity, loyalty, mutual assistance, unconditional solidarity, constancy, generosity, hospitality, and respect for promises, human dignity, and the property of others with strategies for getting rich quickly, for social and economic ascent, and for gaining power. The old values everywhere sustained the ethos of societies where Islam is widespread and brought spiritual gain by focusing all questions of moral conduct on the absoluteness of God. This is true for Arabia itself, where Islam was born, and it can be verified in the other Islamized countries, from Indonesia to Morocco, from Turkey to Senegal.

Old and deeply rooted in individual habit as it is, this ethos, the cement of traditional societies, is no longer externalized except as militant energy in the so-called Islamist movements. That is why it is difficult to analyze with precision the very ambiguous contents of the discourse and behavior of these movements. While the political objective is clear and predominant, the emphasis on ethical and religious motives is never absent. There is surely an investment of a spiritual energy of ethical-religious origin in the revolutionary accomplishments of these movements.

That consideration poses the problem of ethical judgment in contemporary Muslim societies: Using Islamic criteria, can we attribute a moral and religious status to the acts termed "revolutionary" by the agents and their superiors, "terrorist" by the victims? The Muslim jurist-theologians of the period of *ijtihād* would have posed the question in these same terms and in this perspective. I do not see it raised anywhere in our time.

Is this to say that the criterion of efficiency, of pragmatic action, has definitively replaced, as it has in the West, that which al-Ghazali called "the balance of moral action," *mīzān al-'amal*? For sure, the "scientific" appraisal of the circumstances, the conditions for production, of an act tend everywhere to cause the suspension of moral judgment or its complete elimination. This tendency is a sign of our culture and our so-called modern civilization. It is a blindspot of intellectual modernity. In the case of Muslim societies, the abyss is even greater between the multiplication and extension of violent behaviors and the opportunities remaining for intellectuals to counterbalance semantic disorder and the rout of thought. Western democracies provide lots of free space where critical thought and artistic creativity can at least lay stepping stones toward new beginnings of reflection, of knowledge, and of moral, political, and cognitive codes. Moreover, scientific and technological research continually modify the material and moral conditions in which these societies produce their existence. These simultaneous activities have great capacity to integrate and direct. There is nothing equivalent to these processes in contemporary Muslim societies. The Muslim societies import the most complex technological matériel, buy the most sophisticated armaments, and install high-performance laboratories, but at the same time governments exercise such rigorous ideological control that all these instruments of scientific modernity have little perceptible effect on mentalities or even on reflective thought. The capacity to integrate and to progress is transformed into an agent of disintegration and semantic detour.

Some may find this picture of morality and politics in the Islamic world a bit pessimistic or extreme. In fact, I have tried to undertake a diagnosis much more than to give an exhaustive description of all the manifestations and expressions of ethics and politics. In contrast, the Orientalist approach to Muslim societies expressly forgoes diagnosis, because Orientalists decline to interfere in questions that do not concern them as citizens of Western societies.

The Muslim intellectual must today fight on two fronts: one against social science as practiced by Orientalism in a disengaged, narrative, descriptive style; the other against the offensive/defensive apologia of Muslims who compensate for repeated attacks on the "authenticity" and the "identity" of the Islamic personality with dogmatic affirmations and self-confirming discourse. And beyond these two obstacles, always present but at least identifiable, the Muslim intellectual must contribute through the Islamic example to an even more fundamental diagnosis, especially regarding questions of ethics and politics: What are the blindspots, the failings, the non sequiturs, the alienating constraints, the recurrent weaknesses of modernity? Protest must reach every form of activity, every point of intervention, every logical structure. From Hegel to Nietzsche, Enlightenment thought was invoked as the *opposite* of myth in an effort to escape the clutches of religious dogma; at the same time that reason performed this "liberating" critique, it also fell back into a nostalgic celebration of the *origins* of civilization, especially the Greek polis and the first Christian communities, which were the equivalent of the "Pious Elders" among the Muslims.

Scholars get beyond Enlightenment thought by integrating myth—hence the accumulated symbolic capital carried and maintained by religion—into the cognitive activity of reason. The comparative history of religion, conducted within this perspective, furnishes a particularly fertile ground for the elaboration of new kinds of rationality. It goes without saying that forms of religious expression cannot be detached from symbolic and artistic creativity. It is not a matter of extending indefinitely the horizons of meaning open to the scrutiny of reason. Instead of exhausting ourselves in an effort to reclaim contingent values tied to abandoned forms of culture and bygone systems of civilization, scholars today must propose new opportunities for the emancipation, exaltation, and mastery of human existence and for the thought and action of men and women.[6]

Notes

1. Jürgen Habermas, *Le discours philosophique de la modernité* (Paris: Gallimard, 1988).

2. I mean all the ulema as well as a large number of researchers and essayists for whom good taste requires that they take their distance from "Western science."

3. See my *L'humanisme arabe au IVᵉ/IXᵉ siècle: Miskawayh philosophe et historien* (Paris: Vrin, 1970; 2nd ed., 1982).

4. Cited by André Miquel, *La géographie humaine du monde musulman,* vol. 4 (La Haye: Mouton, 1988), pp. 32–33.

5. See my *L'humanisme arabe.*

6. I corrected the proofs of this chapter on January 22, 1991, while the Gulf War was taking so many lives and raising so many passions and so much indignation everywhere in the world. I originally wrote the chapter in July 1990, before the outbreak of the crisis in the Gulf. I nonetheless stick with my critical analysis and my refusal of militant forms of discourse from whatever source. I feel only a need to further radicalize that which I have already written by adding a critique of "Western" reason, which is so sure of itself and of the *right* that it intends to make prevail even though its material and technological hegemony has rendered obsolete, bypassed, and useless all *ethical* considerations. I have not come across many "Western" intellectuals who write or speak, as they should, of the failings of such reason since 1945 and of the even more tragic failings that will surely be apparent *after* the Gulf War. I fear, in fact, that we are returning very quickly to the status quo ante of "international order."

24

Mediterranean Culture

How can scholars most effectively give greater currency in today's most dynamic societies, those bearing most of the burden of change and innovation, to the notion of Mediterranean culture?

Many people have dedicated themselves to cross-cultural exchanges between Muslim and Western societies in domains as diverse as sports (Mediterranean Games), music, dance, architecture, cooking, painting, and literature, not to mention economic interchange, legal and political institutions, technology, and science. But the exchange is always unequal, and the Mediterranean contribution is too often reduced to folk songs and dance, nostalgic evocations, aesthetic appreciation of local peculiarities, and tourist consumption of exotic products. By asking about the most effective means of scholarly activity, I intend expressly to restore equilibria and to modernize archaic attitudes as well as to rehabilitate a sense of the living cultural traditions of Muslim societies in the intellectual and cultural practices of the West.

Scientific research on the history, cultures, and civilization of Mediterranean societies abounds, and yet scholarly knowledge of the Mediterranean world is unbalanced: The societies on the European side are much better understood than the Arab-Muslim countries to the south and east. And what is known about these countries too often depends on the writings of Western scholars. This imbalance makes it urgent that scholars intervene to rectify historical perspectives, fill in substantial gaps, eliminate prejudices and put back together an area that has been blown apart, ripped up, and sharply disputed for centuries. The resurgence of Islam as a powerful factor in the history of societies recently liberated from colonial domination makes research aimed at identifying, revivifying, and rehabilitating Mediterranean culture very topical. The presence in Europe of a significant group of Muslim emigrants sharpens the urgency of generating an open, critical body of knowledge about values common to the whole set of Mediterranean countries.

Visiting villages in Greater Kabylia, a mountainous Berber region of Algeria, one is struck by the brutal eruption of an architecture that borrows both from the style of low-cost French housing projects and that of so-called modern villas. The old low houses made of clay, whitewashed with chalk and topped with gently sloped roofs of typical tile, often dilapidated, betray themselves as leftovers. Their inhabitants have themselves suffered social, economic, and, of course, cultural marginalization. The villages of Andalusia, Sicily, Provence, Mykonos, Rhodes, and Sardinia have stood up better than those of Kabylia, but they have not escaped the constraints of economics, materials, and style imposed from the outside.

One could say the same things about kinship structures, the very old and tenacious code of honor, the status of men and women, the sense of hospitality and of celebration, the areas of social communication and cultural expression, the relationship with the divine, the culture of saintliness, and attachment to the land. In those individual and collective behaviors translating a fund of common values, one can see the processes of disintegration, transformation, and desymbolization under the impact of more efficient, more emancipating, more "modern" norms. The tensions, contrasts, eradications, and marginalizations have not occurred only between the West and Islam, as the discourse of the ideology of combat on the Muslim side and the discourse of hegemony on the Western side would have us believe. The lines of cleavage are much older than that and irremediable between semantic, semiotic, and symbolic universes still insufficiently identified. That is why all timely local actions to save a monument, restore a musical, pictorial, or literary work, or rehabilitate a particular dance, festivity, or source of solidarity seem to me both necessary and insufficient. Such efforts can, in fact, lead to the recomposition of Mediterranean culture only if the relationships between thought and sign and between thought and symbol are radically rethought in the perspective of a comparative history and a philosophical critique of all the cultural and cognitive systems present.

Certain values, practices, behaviors, and traditions always escape the need for this radical critique. I am thinking of music, songs, dances, culinary traditions, artisan activity, and styles and places of social communication. But such manifestations of culture will continue to be extracted from context and turned into folklore, hence thrown backwards into an obsolete past, unless they are integrated into modern systems of knowledge and cultural creation. The more a group remains outside the forces and productive zones of modernity, the more its cultural identity is threatened by disintegration and even disappearance. And the more a group is engaged in the historic process of modernization, the more it is stretched between the need to protect its patrimony and the temptation to break more radically with the weight of a burdensome heritage. In this way gaps emerged between those sacrificed to modernity and the elites who serve "progress." In both cases, the strategies of action remain inadequate.

A culture grows, enriches itself, and spreads when it has precise criteria for the identification of truth, good, and beauty not just for the clan, tribe, group, community, or nation but for the whole of humankind. Greek and religious thought have each taught us about such an ambition. But it has been shown that the logical categories of Aristotle, for example, are linked to the definitions and semantic structures of the Greek language. The revealed religions have tried to go beyond precarious and relative human knowledge by riveting attention and desire on the absoluteness of God. But they, too, have utilized naturally occurring human languages for delivering their messages. Neither Greek thought nor revealed religion has managed to undermine local knowledge and empirical forms of rationality in Mediterranean societies to the point of completely replacing them with one or the other forms of universalist thought. Whatever the debt of current Western scientific thought to local knowledge and global systems of thought originating in the Mediterranean basin, the criteria for the identification of truth, good, and beauty remain uncertain and much debated. Mobility of judgment, multiplicity of modes of thought, method, problematics, and respect for cultural "specificities" thrown up as so many absolutes—these are the distinctive characteristics of modern rationality.

To deepen our understanding of both local Mediterranean cultures and universalist tendencies, I propose to reflect briefly on four possible paths for a modern cognitive strategy:

1. the dialectic of influence and residues;
2. comparativism;
3. creative tension between language, history, and thought;
4. instructive tension between the rational and the imaginary.

Other scholars working from data and within specialties different from my own might wish to change the order of these paths, add others, or discuss the scientific relevance of explanations I am going to propose. No truly fresh viewpoint can be brought to the history of thought and cultures in the Mediterranean region, however, without moving beyond practices bequeathed by the past, whether within Islam, Christianity, or the secular West, and without invoking strategies for violating dogmas and subverting theories and standard definitions.

1. The dialectic of influence and residues permits rectification of historical, sociological, and philosophical perspectives on cultures and currents of thought linked to the Mediterranean region. Scholars customarily consider the sociohistorical field by starting from loci of power such as the state, writing, learned culture, and orthodoxy. This is true for ancient civilizations as well as for more recent ones. The state draws a boundary between the political domain that it effectively controls and always seeks to extend and the forces that resist. Writing contrasts the preeminence and durability of that which is graphically stable with the oral, which is precarious, incoherent, and inferior. Learned culture defines and sets norms for the true, the right, the good, and the beautiful in tandem with economic and social influences exerted in the official, political domain. It contrasts with so-called popular or folk cultures that are repressed, marginalized, and devalued by the choices of the elites. Orthodoxy represents monopoly of control over symbolic goods (official religion) by knowledgeable elites serving the state; any deviation with respect to orthodoxy thus defined is devalued as heresy or sectarianism.

In this summary there are many subjects, notions, concepts, fields of reality, and angles of vision that, once taken into consideration, would permit scholars to revise their knowledge of Mediterranean societies and, at the same time, their tools for thought. The dialectic of influences and residues is at work in all societies and in all groups that reach the threshold of power, beyond which a *center* exists and grows with respect to a *satellite-periphery*. Thus, the French provinces became peripheral as the monarchical and then republican state affirmed its supremacy. All national units have taken shape according to this model of historical action, which assumes anthropological significance.

In the Mediterranean region, from the epoch of ancient dynasties and empires to that of contemporary nations, numerous and varied ethnocultural groups have been reduced to residual status. The term "residue" is tied dialectically to that of influence, but this in no way implies a Manichean contrast between the good, on the side of the dominated, and the bad, on the side of constituted, dominant powers. I am speaking of an analytical approach that restores a voice to all social actors independently of their positions with respect to the scale of political, economic, cultural, and religious values prescribed by the centralizing state. Thus, the broader, more inclusive concept of symbolic capital must replace the notion of orthodoxy as defined by the clerics and applied by the secular arm. Symbolic capital is to be found in the revealed religions turned official as well as in the religions regarded as pagan and hence "false" according to the dogmatic perspective of speculative theologies. The recurrent force of orthodoxy as an instrument of control over ideological deviation can only be mastered by shifting the problematics of true and false, correctness and heresy, good and evil, participation in the political activity of the state and protest.

From such an approach would follow a new and radical liberation of all forms of cultural expression linked to linguistic, religious, economic, and ethnic diversity of groups coexisting in a single political space controlled by a center. The liberation would affect not only the present and the future of these groups—such as Corsicans, Basques, Catalans, Occitans, Sicilians, Cypriots, Berbers, Kurds, and Armenians—but also the writing of the history of winning cultures and marginalized cultures.

It would be interesting, for example, to reread the work of Ibn Khaldun, so innovative in his time, in the light of concepts and methods required by the dialectic of influences and residues. Ibn Khaldun surely perceived and described an aspect of that dialectic in the Maghrib by distinguishing "the civilization of the desert" (bedouins, who had been called *a'rāb* in the Qur'an) from the emancipating civilization of the Islamic state, agriculture, sedentary rural life, learned culture, and orthodoxy, of which Ibn Khaldun was himself a perfect representative and agent. By reviving his analyses without extending them and opening them to the critique of ideologies, contemporary historians and sociologists, starting with E. F. Gautier, have perpetuated the center's simplistic view of peripheral cultures.

For the future of the Mediterranean region, it is still more enlightening to take up the dialectic of influences and residues for that privileged historic moment represented by the appearance of the Qur'an and the decisive activity of the Prophet Muhammad. Indeed, with the emergence of the Qur'an, former influences such as the Arab pantheon, the Meccan aristocracy, the poetic Koine, and clan solidarities came to be challenged as part of the *jāhiliyya,* while new influences, such as the community-state of Medina, the *'ilm* or symbolic capital of the Qur'an, and the scriptures in the double sense of revealed *Book* and written *book* (*muṣḥaf*), rapidly asserted themselves, nourishing a learned culture and generating an orthodoxy. Then the imperial moment (dominated by the Umayyads and Abbasids) quickly succeeded the Qur'anic moment and accentuated the dialectic of influences and residues in all Mediterranean societies. The new Muslim influences encountered resistance in the face of precisely parallel influences directed by Byzantium, the Christian West, the Spanish Reconquista, bourgeois capitalism, and today's industrial civilization and high technology.

2. The worthy efforts, the initial explorations, and the insufficiencies of scholars who have tried since the nineteenth century to master the discipline of comparative literature are well known. Academic specialization and the breakdown of what was once the unifying effect of thought have prevented comparativism from spreading to theology, philosophy, law, historiography, folklore, religious beliefs, rites, kinship structures—in short, to the various levels at which culture manifests itself in each linguistic area. Even for literature, comparativism has scarcely gone beyond the confines of the great Western languages.[1]

Pierre Bourdieu, who attempted to stake out boundaries between the intellectual and religious domains, has not managed to show how the two domains connect or how they resonate with each other and with other domains of social and historical reality. There is a move being sketched toward a typology of domains of cultural activity based on identifying distinctive traits. That research is still at the level of description and taxonomy. But the more difficult problem of generating a topology of meaning has scarcely been approached. By that I mean creating space for the emergence and construction of notions, concepts, and categories to be found in all types of culture and in all domains of semantic and semiotic activity. I am thinking of the much debated and omnipresent questions of myth, mythology, mythologization; transcendence and transcendentalization; the holy, the saintly, sacralization, and desacralization; spiritualism, spiritualization, and mystification; the profane, the secular, and the secularized; symbol, sign, and signal; reason, rationality, imagination, and imaginary.

These key notions are indispensable tools of any comparativism. They are *upstream* from analyses and classifications of particular cultures. I am perfectly aware that, to work with these concepts, one must constantly go from the local to the global and vice versa, as Clifford Geertz in particular has shown.[2] In the Mediterranean region, there are numerous pockets of local knowledge surviving the expansion and domination of global knowledge. They warrant reexamination and rehabilitation of the type that Hassan Fathy has tried to do for architecture in Egypt and Marcel Pagnol did not so long ago for Provençal literature in France.

By enlarging the fields of vision for knowledge and culture, comparativism will deliver us from becoming trapped in narrow particularisms and outmoded conservatism, at the same time favoring the exchange of ideas, works, practices, and values among repressed and forgotten cultural identities, the great traditional cultures linked to revealed religions, and the all-powerful culture termed modern, which for the first time in history has overturned the initial basis of all culture and knowledge:

the *relationship of mind to signs.* The mind wants to dominate this relationship by constructing a critical *relationship,* more and more rigorous, between its own psychological configuration, on the one hand (the respective roles of reason, intellect, imagination, imaginary, memory, affectivity), and the world of objective reference points mediated by signs, on the other. A revolution is affecting the modern sense of *being-in-the-world.* We moderns are leaving behind the stage of natural, immediate immersion in a universe abounding in signs, which are absorbed and invested in the most diverse semiological structures—from the most modest piece of furniture to the most imposing monument, from the briefest of proverbs to the books of revelation. Today semiotic analysis labors to deconstruct such structures.

Certainly local and traditional cultures of the Mediterranean world cannot fend off the mutations taking place in the way human beings insert themselves into the world any better than other cultures can. The relevance of a cultural response to this tendency, which hurls the mind toward a new destiny, emerges sharper than ever when one considers the social and ideological power of what has come to be called the return of the religious, especially in the Islamic and Jewish camps. Instead of reflecting upon the radical breakdown that all cultures are undergoing, Islamic thought claims historical and doctrinal continuity with the founding moment when the divine calling of human beings was revealed. Only the comparative history of revealed religions can elucidate and advance the endless discussions triggered by these claims. It happens that research of this sort ranks among the most neglected areas of study in all universities and institutes, whether on the Western or the Muslim side.

I am not proposing a mere comparison of Judaism, Christianity, and Islam as religious traditions. Theological and philosophical thought developed with respect to these traditions must also become the object of modern, critical investigation. At present, the teaching of theology is confined to religious establishments, while departments of philosophy continue to stride through a thousand years in the history of ideas, moving from classical Greece to Descartes, Liebniz, and Spinoza, then to Kant and Heidegger. Even the newer universities, such as those in Arab countries, have not emphasized the teaching of medieval philosophy in Jewish, Christian, and Islamic settings. However, a more profound, comparative knowledge of the great streams of thought born and developed in the Mediterranean region would shed new light on current cleavages between the temporal and the spiritual, between secularism and religion, and between secular modernity and living religious traditions.

3. The history of ideas long ago separated ideas from the languages transporting them and from the histories generating them—the histories to which they, in turn, contribute. What is more, the general history of groups and societies marginalized by imperial or national states has been written by elites using the great languages of civilization, such as Greek, Latin, Arabic, French, and English. Ethnographers have themselves reinforced this tendency by confining themselves to the study of dialects distinct from the great official languages. Jesus spoke Aramaic in Palestine, but his message was very quickly consigned to Greek and then commented upon and diffused in Latin, before the emergence of European languages. While Arabic under-

went rapid and extensive expansion from the seventh to the eleventh centuries, the competition of Persian, Turkish, and then modern languages—particularly French and English—created a gap between religious, learned language, on the one hand, and living dialects, on the other. These dialects continue to be neglected; in the Arab nations, this has been so especially since the necessity of constructing national units dictated the choice of standard Arabic as the official language.

This situation entailed grave consequences for the livelihood of so-called popular cultures in the whole Mediterranean basin. Access to these cultures depends upon bibliographies and archives prepared in national languages as much on the European side as on the Arab-Islamic side. Therefore, historians and sociologist-anthropologists today face the question of reassembling the Mediterranean cultural area. One must come back to what survives of languages, customs, rights, beliefs, literatures, agrarian practices, and artisan enterprise in those regions heretofore protected by their geographical situation, whether on islands, in mountains, or on deserts. Djerba, Mzab, Djurdjura, and the Aurès are examples in Tunisia and Algeria.

The theoretical position by which one would refuse to separate language, history, and thought when attempting to penetrate the culture of a group and interpret it correctly can be applied a fortiori to the cultures of the great languages currently dominating the Mediterranean region: Arabic, Hebrew, Greek, Italian, Spanish, and French. The intellectual and scientific hegemony of these languages is directly tied to the history of political and economic competition around the Mediterranean basin. That fact creates new problems of access to cultures and societies, particularly those expressing themselves in Arabic. I am thinking here of the role played by Orientalism since the nineteenth century, of the impact of French on the Maghrib and that of English on the Near East, of the position of Arab- and Berber-speaking emigrants in Europe and of literature produced by French-speaking Maghribians, and of unequal interchange between the Arabic-speaking and French-speaking worlds.

In contemporary Arab and Islamic discourse, one often hears denunciations of the "cultural aggression" of the West (*al-ghazw al-fikrī*). Beyond ideological tensions and sterile polemics, surely peace among peoples living on the shores of the Mediterranean will arrive via reconsideration of cultural interchange and linguistic communication within nations as well as among nations. Right now, as efforts, attention, and volition are turned toward the unification of Europe, scholars must be careful not to accentuate the isolation and dependence of Arab and Islamic nations, which by virtue of belonging to the Mediterranean region are capable of enriching and energizing the European domain that is in the process of emerging.

The relationship of the mind to its own activity is in the process of change as a result of scientific progress and the acceleration of cultural exchange. Reason questions its own status in the psychological configuration of the mind and, certainly, in the unfolding of all cognitive activity. Scholars must thus revise their images of so-called archaic, traditional, and modern cultures, their attitudes toward cultural interchange, and their practices within the logosphere defining each language.

The rational and the imaginary must assume more flexible definitions and more realistic functions in cognitive activity and cultural production. Reason must give up its arrogant sovereignty and recognize the portion of imagination to be found in its most rigorous exercises, especially in the domain of the human and social sciences. The social imaginary, broadly open to irrational and mythological elements required by political life and religious traditions, has gained recognition as one of the psychological realms where convictions, beliefs, representations, and images of reality are organized into a dynamic vision endowed with its own coherence and capable of animating individual and collective behavior. The mobilizing discourse of prophets, saints, heroes, leaders, kings, presidents, and preachers resonates in the social imaginary. The ideal images stored in the imaginary and reactivated by representative leaders unleash great revolutionary movements.

In what way does psychosocial power so defined influence my reflections on Mediterranean culture? Does not its anthropological and psychological influence extend to all cultures in all kinds of societies?

The rational and the imaginary are two interdependent aspects of any cognitive action undertaken by the mind, and they exist in fruitful tension with each other. By recognizing this fact, scholars can free themselves from dichotomous thought, which has long pitted reason against imagination, *logos* against *muthos,* concept against metaphor, proper meaning against figurative meaning, science against religion, diverse beliefs against superstitions, religion against magic, modern against archaic or traditional, civilized against primitive, developed against underdeveloped. (This final contrast is the last metamorphosis of dichotomous, imperial thought.)

By such means scholars provide themselves with the intellectual tools for reinterpreting all streams of our cultural heritage. In the current context of struggle for economic hegemony and political domination, these streams tend to reappear under such names as identity, authenticity, and personality. These names cannot disguise the customary operations of the apologetic and ideological exploitation of culture. As a result, an indispensable, critical reexamination of the whole heritage is delayed, and the delay encourages the development of misunderstandings and tensions like those dividing Islam and Europe, the Arab world and the West, ever since new political, strategic, and economic stakes have emerged in the Mediterranean.

The aspiration to hegemony is always linked to an affirmation of truth that excludes competing truths. Dogmatic, sovereign reason, with great confidence and even arrogance, achieves this work of dividing up and hiding the real stakes of the competition. In this way, it produces an imaginary of rationality authorized either by political or religious discourse, depending on the social and cultural strata to be mobilized. By insisting on this constant intrusion of the imaginary and thus imposing tolerance and modesty upon reason, the human and social sciences make possible greater lucidity.

In a book entitled *The Detour,*[3] Georges Balandier provides a significant example of this new mission for scientific reason. After a long and patient journey through societies of black Africa, the sociologist-anthropologist comes back to the society and culture of his origins and subjects them to the same analytical, critical examination. He demonstrates that the West, according itself permission to interpret other cultures with the help of a kind of reason cleansed of all mythology, is as much conditioned by the social imaginary as traditional, conservative, and archaic societies are. Hence scholars must speak, as does Balandier, of anthropo-*logics* and, for varieties of thought that see themselves as faithful to religious sources, of theo-anthropo-*logics*. Scholars must respect the importance of meanings and directions of thought suggested by the plural: The new states of rationality are attached to this plural.

In 1536 the treaty signed between Francis I and Suleiman the Magnificent against the power of Charles V consecrated the importance of rivalry in the Mediterranean. Fernand Braudel located the great break marking the end of Ottoman strategic and economic primacy in 1650 or even 1680. Already in 1571, the battle of Lepanto had gravely affected Ottoman influence. 'Uluj 'Ali, a Neapolitan who had ruled Algiers and then become an admiral of the Ottoman navy, died in 1587, and the reign of Philip II, who had installed himself in Lisbon from 1580 to 1583, ended in 1598.

The historic metamorphoses of strategies for dominating the Mediterranean have never destroyed the sociocultural bases of unity in the Mediterranean world: a severe code of honor that prescribes vendetta and maintains women in an unfavorable position,[4] primitive tools, archaic agricultural techniques, an inflexible patriarchy, cities shaped by climate and the sea, a style of life and communication in which warm and spontaneous sociability takes precedence.

The cultural bifurcation initiated by industrial civilization has for the first time affected the traditional solidarities, the relationship to the land and to the symbolic capital[5] that have perpetuated for centuries a characteristic universe of thought, action, and existence. What does the Mediterranean world lose and what does it gain in this historic adventure undertaken by a civilization that is so expressly indebted to the great outbursts of creative thought in Mesopotamia, Palestine, Egypt, Arabia, Greece, Italy, Spain, and France?

The peoples of the Mediterranean have responded to this question with the help of new historic initiatives. Will the refusal issued by political Islam to the aggressive aspects of the conquering West[6] contribute to the reaffirmation of a reassembled, active Mediterranean, or will it hasten the breakup of the world and the end of the region's mission? The quality of civilization in gestation rides on that question. The current confrontation between Islam and the West must be perceived, conducted, and lived in the perspective of this fight for the meaning of human existence begun by the prophets and pursued by the saints, heroes, thinkers, and creators at the heights of Mediterranean culture.

Notes

1. I have not succeeded even recently in convincing my colleagues at the New Sorbonne (Paris III) of the need to create a chair in Mediterranean literatures in the Department of General and Comparative Literature.

2. Clifford Geertz, *Local Knowledge: Further Essays in Interpretive Anthropology* (New York: Basic, 1983).

3. Georges Balandier, *Le détour: pouvoir et modernité* (Paris: Fayard, 1985).

4. See Christiane Souriau, ed., *Femmes et politique autour de la Méditerranée* (Paris: L'Harmattan, 1980).

5. About this key concept, see Pierre Bourdieu, *Le sens pratique* (Paris: Minuit, 1980).

6. The notion of the West covers more than Europe; the United States and especially Japan have their places (as will Korea and other financial and industrial powers in the near future), as we know, in the control and development of technology and in the whole of material civilization.

Glossary

adab culture, the humanities, humanism

afḍal better, excellent

'ahd pact, covenant

aḥkām principles, rules, regulations

ahl al-dhikr those who invoke God; Sufis

ahl al-'iṣma wal-'adāla those who profess the infallibility of the imam and justice

ahl al-kitāb people of the Book

ahl al-sunna wal-jamā'a those who follow tradition and the community

al-ahwāl al-shakhsiyya personal statute

al-a'imma al-mujtahidūn those specialists capable of *ijtihād*

al-ākhira the life beyond, the other life

'ālim, 'ulamā' (pl.) ulema, learned person, expert

a'mal good works

anā-l-ḥaqq I am God/Truth

'aqīda profession of faith

a'rāb bedouins (as used in the Qur'an)

'arsh throne

asāṭīr al-awwalīn legends of the founders

asbāb al-nuzūl moments of opportunity, circumstances of revelation

aṣl, uṣūl (pl.) source, foundation

āya sign-symbol, a single unity of interpretation in the Qur'anic text

a'yān leaders, notables

'ayn choice, prime

'ayyārūn outlaws who enroll in the *futūwa*, or militias

banu ādam sons (descendents) of Adam

baraka blessing, effusion of holiness

al-bashar humankind

bāṭin inner, intrinsic, hidden

bid'a innovation

blād al-makhzan domain of the state

blād al-siba domain of rebellion

al-ḍaḥiyya sacrifice

dakhīla foreign, extraneous

dār al-ḥarb land of war

dār al-ḥikma house of wisdom

dār al-islām land of Islam

da'wa   call, summons to belief

dawla   dynasty, state power

al-dhikr   invocation of the names of God; Sufi ritual

dhimmī   protected peoples

dīn   religion

dīn al-ḥaqq   true religion

al-dunyā   this world; life in this world, as opposed to *al-ākhira*

faḍl   surplus, matter of secondary importance

fatāwā   formal legal rulings or opinions (sing. *fatwā*)

fiqh   jurisprudence

firaq   sects, confessional groups

al-firqa al-nājiya   the community promised salvation

al-fitna-l-kubrā   the great sedition; the civil war pitting the fourth caliph, 'Ali, against
      Mu'awiya

al-furqān   the discriminating proof; revelation

furū'   branches, laws derived from *uṣūl* (foundations)

futūwa   youthful militias used to maintain moral and social order

al-ghazw al-fikrī   cultural aggression

ḥajj   pilgrimage

ḥukm allah   divine rule, sentence

ḥulūl   incarnation, impersonation

ḥuqūq allah   rights of God

'ibādāt   obligations, religious observances

ijtihād   intellectual effort, independent judgment in a legal or theological question

'ilm   science, true and illuminating knowledge

imān   faith

insān   human being

'ird   code of honor

ishrāq   illuminism, mysticism

islām   attitude of obedience toward God

isnād   chains of authorities or witnesses for hadiths

istinbāṭ al-aḥkām   derivation of legal rules from sacred texts

ittiḥād   unification

jāhiliyya   state of ignorance; pre-Islamic times

jinn   good or evil spirit

jizya   tax on non-Muslims

ka'ba   black cube at the center of the mosque in Mecca

kalimatu-llah   Word of God

khalīfa, khulafā'   (pl.) successor, caliph

al-khāṣṣa   elites

khatm al-anbiya   seal of the prophets

al-kitāb   the Book

kun   fiat

kutub al-milal wal-niḥal   books on confessions and creeds, that is, heresiography

lā ḥukma illā li-llāh   there is no authority but that of God *lā yamussuhu illā-l-muṭahharūn*   it (the Book) is touched only by the clean

mahdī   rightly guided

mamlaka   kingdom

matn   the text of a hadith, as opposed to its *isnād*

mawālī   clients, allies, helpers; new converts to Islam

miḥrāb   prayer niche in mosques indicating the direction of Mecca

mirabilia   the miracles of nature

mīthāq   alliance, pact, covenant

mīzān al-'amal   balance of moral action

mu'amalāt   worldly transactions, mutual relations

mufti   counselor in Islamic law

muḥaddithūn   those devoted to hadith, hadith folk

muḥkamāt   explicit verses (of the Qur'an)

mukhtalaq   apocryphal, contrived, false

mulūk   kings

mu'minūn   believers, faithful

munāfiqūn   hypocrites, dissemblers

munāzarāt   competition, confrontations

murīdūn   disciples, novices of a Sufi order

muṣḥaf   Closed Official Corpus, the Qur'an

mushrikūn   polytheists

muslim   Muslim, one who obeys God

mutakallimūn   theologians

mutashābihāt   ambiguous verses (of the Qur'an)

al-nabiyy al-'ummī   the prophet before he was introduced to revelation

nafs   soul, mind, life, personal identity

nahḍa   rebirth, renaissance, Arab revival

naqliyya   traditional

al-nās   the people

al-nāsikh wal-mansūkh   that which abrogates and that which is abrogated

al-qādiriyya   profession of faith asserting free will

qalb   heart

qara'a   to read, recite

al-qaṣaṣ   mythical tale

qibla   direction of Mecca, focus of all eyes

qira'āt   readings, recitations

qiṣaṣ   mythical tale

qiyās   analogy, measure

qul   to say, speak

al-qur'ān   the reciting; the Qur'an (Koran, Coran)

risāla   letters

rūḥ   spirit, breath

al-ṣaḥīḥān   the two authentic compilations of hadith

al-salaf al-ṣāliḥ   the venerable forefathers

salafī   the Islamic reform movement founded by Muhammad 'Abdu in Egypt *shahāda*   profession of faith

sharī'a   *shari'a*, religious law

shaykh   sheik, spiritual or tribal leader

shi'i   Shi'ite

al-shurāt   those who sacrifice their lives for God

sīra   biography of the Prophet

ṣūfī   Sufi, mystic

sulṭān   political power, sultan

sulūk   course, comportment

sunna   practice, custom of the Prophet

taḍmīn   implicit

tafsīr   exegesis, commentary

ṭāghūt   idol, a false god

tahdhīb al-akhlāq   treatise on ethics

tanzīl   descent, revelation

taqdīr   implied

ta'ṣīl   establishing a firm foundation

turāth   cultural legacy of the classical age

'ulūm 'aqliyya   rational sciences

'ulūm dīniyya   religious sciences

'ulūm naqliyya   traditional sciences

umma   community

umm al-kitāb   the Heavenly Book

umma Muḥammadiyya   Muhammad's community

uṣūl   sources, foundations

uṣūl al-fiqh   sources, foundations of law

usṭūra   legend or fable, fabulous story

al-waḥda   unity

waḥdat al-wujūd   oneness of existence

waḥy   revelation

wālī   marabouts

yaqūlu allah   God says

ẓāhir   manifest, clear, apparent

zakāt   alms tax, charity

zāwiya, zawāyā   (pl.) small mosque, place where religious teaching occurs

ẓulumāt   shadows

ẓulumāt al-jāhiliyya   shadows of ignorance, of the pre-Islamic age

Other Works by Mohammed Arkoun

Books

Actualité d'une culture mediterraneéne. Tampere, Finland: Institute for Peace Research, 1990.

Architectural Alternatives in Deteriorating Societies. Geneva: Aga Khan Trust, 1992.

Aspects de la pensée musulmane classique. Paris: IPN, 1963.

The Concept of Revelation: From Ahl al-Kitāb to the Societies of the Book. Occasional Papers, Claremont Graduate School, 1988.

Essais sur la pensée islamique. Paris: Maisonneuve et Larose, 1973; 3rd ed., 1984.

L'ethique musulmane d'après Mawardi. Paris: P. Geuthner, 1964.

Al-fikr al-islāmiyy: qirā'a 'ilmiyya (translation of various essays first published in French). Beirut: Markaz al-Inma al-Qawmi, 1986.

L'humanisme arabe au IVᵉ/Xᵉ siècle: Miskawayh philosophe et historien. Paris: Vrin, 1970; 2nd ed., 1982.

L'Islam. Hier, demain (with L. Gardet). Paris: Burchet-Chastel, 1978; 2nd ed., 1982; partially translated into Arabic by Hachem Salah as *Al-islām: aṣāla wa mumārasa,* Beirut: Dar al-Tanwir, 1983.

L'Islam, morale et politique. Paris: UNESCO, Desclée de Brouwer, 1986; translated into Arabic by Hachem Salah as *Al-islam al-akhlāq wal-siyāsa,* Beirut: Markaz al-Inma al-Qawmi, 1990.

Al-islām: naqd wa-jtihād. Beirut: Dar al-Saqi, 1990; 2nd ed., 1992.

L'Islam, religion et société (with M. Arosio and M. Borrmans). Paris: Editions du Cerf, 1982; Italian version, Turin: Cidizioni RAI Radiotelevisione Italiana, 1980.

Islam e Società. Torino: ERI, 1980; translated into French as *Islam: religion et société,* Paris: Cerf, 1982.

Lectures du Coran. Paris: Maisonneuve et Larose, 1982; 2nd ed., Tunis: Alif, 1991.

Min al-ijtihād ila naqd al-'aql al-islamī. London: Dar al-Saqi, 1991.

Min fayṣal al-tafriqa ilā faṣl al-maqāl: 'ayna huwa al-fikr al-islāmiyya al-mu'āsir (translation by Hachem Salah of essays originally published in French, with an introduction composed in Arabic). Beirut: Dar al-Saqi, 1992.

Les musulmans: Consultation islamo-chrétienne entre Muhammed Arkoun [et al.] et Youakim Moubarac. Paris: Beauchesne, 1971.

Ouvertures sur l'Islam. Paris: J. Grancher, 1989; 2nd ed., 1992.

Pélérinage à la Mecque (with Azzedine Guellouz and Abdelaziz Frikha). Tunis: Sud Editions, 1977.

La pensée arabe. Paris: Presses universitaires de France, 1975; 4th ed., 1991; translated into Arabic as *Al-fikr al-'arabiyy,* Beirut: Dar al-Saqi, 1990; into English as *Arab Thought,* New Delhi: S. Chand, 1988.

Pour une critique de la raison islamique. Paris: Maisonneuve et Larose, 1984.

Rethinking Islam Today. Occasional Papers Series, Center for Contemporary Arab Studies, Georgetown University, 1987.

Tārīkhiyyāt al-fikr al-'arabiyy al-islāmiyy (translation of various essays first published in French). Beirut: Markaz al-Imma al-Qawmi, 1986.

Traité d'ethique: traduction française avec introduction et notes du Tahdhib al-akhlāq de Miskawayh. Damascus: Institut Français, 1969; 2nd ed., 1988.

Articles

"Actualité d'ibn Rushd musulman," in *Multiple Averroës,* edited by Jean Jolinet. Paris: Les Belles Lettres, 1978.

"Actualité du problème de la personne dans la pensée islamique," in *Revue internationale des sciences sociales.* Paris: UNESCO, 1988.

"The Adequacy of Contemporary Islam to the Political, Social and Economic Development of North Africa," *Africa Studies Quarterly* 4:1–2 (1982).

"Algérie 1993: réflexions sur un destin historique," *Revue du monde musulman et de la Meditérranée* 65 (1993).

"Les Arabes vus par le Professeur J. Berque," *Esprit,* no. 1 (1975).

"Avec Mouloud Mammeri à Taourirt-Mimoun," in *Litterature et oralité au Maghrib: Hommage a Mouloud Mammeri,* edited by Charles Bonn. Paris: L'Harmattan, 1993.

"Comment situer l'Islam dans l'histoire récente?" in *Enciclopedia del Novecento.* Milan: Il Quadrato, 1985.

"Le concept de société du Livre-livre," in *Interpréter: hommage à Claude Geffré,* edited by Jean-Pierre Jossua and Nicholas-Jean Sed. Paris: Cerf, 1992.

"The Concept of Authority in Islamic Thought," in *Essays in Honour of Bernard Lewis.* Princeton: Princeton University Press, 1989.

"Construction et signification dans le monde islamique: introduction théorique au Prix Aga Khan d'Architecture," *Mimar* 7 (1983).

"De la stratégie de domination à une coopération créatrice entre l'Europe et le Monde Arabe," in *Le dialogue euro-arabe,* edited by J. Bourrinet. Paris: Economica, 1979.

"De l'Ijtihad à la critique de la Raison islamique: l'exemple du statut de la femme dans la sha-ri'a," in *Algérie, passé, présent et avenir.* Paris: Centre Culturel Algérien, 1990.

"Deux médiateurs de la pensée médiévale: Averroës et Maïmonides," *Courrier de l'UNESCO* (September 1986).

"Le dialogue euro-arabe; essai d'évaluation critique," in *Coopération euro-arabe: diagnostic et prospective,* edited by Bichna Khader. Louvain-la-Neuve, 1982.

"Discours islamiques, discours orientalistes et pensée scientifique," in *As Others See Us: Mutual Perceptions, East and West,* edited by Bernard Lewis. New York: International Society for the Comparative Study of Civilizations, 1985.

"Le droit 'dit' musulman en contexte moderne," in *L'immigration face aux lois de la République,* edited by Edwige Rude Antoine. Paris: Karthala, 1992.

"Les droits de l'homme en Islam," *Recherches et documents du Centre Thomas More* 44 (1984).

"Emergences et problèmes dans le monde musulman contemporain," *Islamo-christiana* 12 (1986); Italian version in the *Enciclopedia italiana,* 1989, under "Islamismo."

"E possible parlare di un umanesimo islamico?" in *L'Opera al Rosso*. Monferrato: Marietti, 1992.

"L'expansion de l'Islam dans la Méditerranée occidentale," *Revue de l'Occident musulman et de la Mediterranée*, no. 1 (1976).

"Les expressions de l'Islam," *Encyclopedia Universalis*, Supplement for 1983.

"Fondments arabo-islamiques de la culture maghrébine," *Franzosische Heute*, no. 2 (1984).

"Les fondements arabo-islamiques de la culture maghrébine," *Gli interscambi culturali*, Proceedings of the International Congress in Amalfi, December 5–8, 1983, Naples, 1986.

"Les horizons de la pensée arabe classique," *Courier de l'UNESCO* (1977).

"Imaginaire social et leaders dans le monde musulman contemporain," *Arabica* 35 (1988).

"Introduction," in *Javidan Khirad* by Ibn Miskawayh. Tehran: Danishgah- Mak Gil, 1976.

"L'Islam, organisation, règles et pouvoirs," *Awraq* (1990).

"Islam, pensée, histoire, l'Orientalisme," *Peuples méditerranéens* 50 (1990).

"Islam, révélation et révolutions," *Dieux en Sociétés*, Autrement, 127 (1992).

"L'Islam actuel devant sa tradition," *Aspects de la foi de l'Islam*. Brussels: Facultes universitaires Saint-Louis, 1985.

"Islam and the Hegemony of the West," in *God, Truth and Reality, Essays in Honour of John Hick*, edited by Arvind Sharma. New York: St. Martin's, 1993.

"L'Islam dans l'histoire," *Maghreb-Machreq* 102 (1983).

"L'Islam davant la Gritica Moderna, l'Hegemonia de l'Occident," *l'Avenç* 46 (1991).

"L'Islam devant les sciences humaines," *Concilium* 116 (1976).

"L'Islam et la laïcité," *Bulletin du Centre Thomas More* 24 (1987). Translated into Arabic as *Al-'almaniyya wal-dīn*, London: Dar al-Saqi, 1990.

"L'Islam et les problèmes du développement," in *Communauté musulmane: 18ᵉ congrès juif mondial*. Paris: Presses universitaires de France, 1978.

"L'Islam et l'historicité," in *Conscience chrétienne et conscience musulmane devant les problèmes du développement*. Tunis: 1976.

"L'Islam face à la modernité," in *Le modèle de l'Occident: 1f colloque d'intellectuels juifs de langue française du congrès juif mondial*. Paris: Presses universitaires de France, 1977.

"L'Islam face aux sciences religieuses," in *Le grand atlas des religions*. Paris: Encyclopaedia universalis, 1988.

"L'Islam face aux sciences religieuses," in *Le grand atlas des religions*. Paris: Encyclopaedia universalis, 1991.

"Islamic Culture, Modernity, Architecture," in *Architecture Education in the Islamic World*. Geneva: The Aga Khan Award for Architecture, 1986.

"Islamic Cultures, Developing Societies, Modern Thought," in *Expressions of Islam in Buildings*. Geneva: Aga Khan Trust, 1990.

"Al-Islām wal-hadātha," in *Al-islām wal-hadātha*. Beirut: Dar al-Saqi, 1990.

"Kémalisme dans une perspective islamique," *Diogène* 127 (1984).

"Lire la ville africaine contemporaine," in *Actes du Colloque de Dakar*. Aga Khan Award for Architecture, 1983.

"Manifestations of Arab Thought in Western Islam," *Diogène* 93 (1976).

"The Meaning of Cultural Conservation in Muslim Societies," in *Architecture and World Conservation in the Islamic World*. Geneva: Aga Khan Trust for Culture, 1991.

"La Méditerranée: une approche multi-rivages," *L'evènement européen* (1988).

"Le IXe séminaire de la pensée islamique à Tlemcen," *Revue de l'Occident musulman et de la Mediterranée* 70 (1976).

"New Perspectives for a Jewish-Christian-Muslim Dialogue," *Journal of Ecumenical Studies* 26:3 (1989).

"The Notion of Revelation: From Ahl al-Kitāb to the Societies of the Book," in *Die Welt des Islam.* (1988).

"Origines islamiques des droits de l'homme," *Revue des sciences morales et poliques*, no. 1 (1989).

"La peine de mort et la torture dans la pensée islamique," *Concilium* 140 (1987).

"Pensiero Religioso e Pensiero Scientifico Nel Contesto Islamico," in *La Passione del Conoscere*, edited by Lorena Preta. Rome-Bari: Laterza, 1993.

"La perception arabe de l'Europe," *Awraq* 10 (1989).

"La place et les fonctions de l'histoire dans la culture arabe," in *Histoire et diversité des cultures.* Paris: UNESCO, 1984.

"Positivisme et tradition dans une perspective islamique: Le cas du kémalisme," *Diogène* 127 (July-September 1984).

"Pour une sociologie de l'échec et de la réussite dans la pensée islamique: l'example d'Ibn Rushd," in *Le choc Averroës: Comment les philosophes ont fait l'Europe*, special edition of *Internationale de l'imaginaire*, 17–18 (1991).

"Preface," in *Le Coran*, translated by Kasimirski. Paris: Flammarion, 1970.

"Le problème des influences en histoire culturelle, d'après l'exemple arabo-islamique," in *Lumières arabes sur l'Occident médiéval*, edited by Henri Loucel and André Miguel. Paris: Anthropos, 1978.

"Propositions pour une autre pensée religieuse," *Islamochristiana*, no. 4 (1987).

"Quelques réflexions sur les difficiles relations entre les musulmans et les chrétiens," *Revue de l'Institut Catholique de Paris* (1982).

"Reflexions d'un musulman sur le 'nouveau' catechisme," *Revue des deux mondes* (April 1993).

"La religion et la paix," in *Entretiens écologiques, Cahiers*, 1979.

"Une rencontre islamo-chrétienne en Tunisie," *Maghreb-Machreq* 69 (1975).

"Les sciences de l'homme et de la société appliquées à l'étude de l'Islam," in *Les sciences sociales aujourd'hui.* Algiers: University of Oran, 1986.

"Se puede Hablar De Un Retorno Del 'Moro' en España," in *Preface à Immigracion Magrebi en España*, edited by Bernabe Lopezyotros. Madrid: Mapfre, 1993.

"Society, State and Religion in Algeria (1962–1985)," in *The Politics of Islamic Revivalism*, edited by Shireen T. Hunter. Bloomington: Indiana University Press, 1988.

"Les tâches de l'intellectuel musulman," in *Intellectuels et militants dans le monde islamique VIIe-XXe s. Cahiers de la Méditerranée*, 1988.

"The Topicality of the Problem of the Person in Islamic Thought," *International Social Science Journal* 117 (August 1988).

"L'unité de l'homme dans la pensée islamique," *Diogène* 140 (1987).

"The Unity of Man in Islamic Thought," translated by R. Scott Walker, *Diogène* 140.

"Les villages socialistes en Algerie," in *Villages socialistes en Afrique*, edited by Alberto Arecchi. Dakar, 1982.

" 'Westliche' Vernunft Kontra 'Islamische' Vernunft? Versuch einer Kritischen Annäherung," in *Der Islam in Auglanch? Perspektiven der Arabichen Welt*, edited by Michel Lüders. Munich: Pipe, 1992.

About the Book and Author

A Berber from the mountainous region of Algeria, Mohammed Arkoun is an internationally renowned scholar of Islamic thought. In this book, he advocates a conception of Islam as a stream of experience encompassing majorities and minorities, Sunni and Shi'a, popular mystics and erudite scholars, ancient heroes and modern critics. A product of Islamic culture, Arkoun nonetheless disagrees with the Islamic establishment and militant Islamist groups; as a student of twentieth-century social science in the West and an admirer of liberalism, he self-consciously distances himself from Western Orientalists and Western conceptions of liberalism.

This book—the first of Arkoun's works to be widely available in English—presents his responses to twenty-four deceptively simple questions, including: Can one speak of a scientific understanding of Islam in the West or must one rather talk about the Western way of imagining Islam? What do the words "Islam," "Muslim," and "Qur'an" mean? What is meant by "revelation" and "tradition"? What did Islam retain from the previously revealed religions—Judaism and Christianity? What did it retain from the religions and customs of pre-Islamic Arabia? In answering these and other questions, Arkoun provides an introduction to one of the world's great religions and offers a biting, radical critique of Islamology as it has been practiced in both East and West.

This is a book for the beginning student of Islam and for the general reader uneasy with media images of Islam as a monolithic, anti-Western, violence-prone religion. It is also a book for specialists seeking an entrée into Arkoun's methodology—his efforts to apply contemporary thinking about anthropology, philosophy, semiotics, history, and sociology to the Islamic tradition and its relationship to the West. It is a book for anyone concerned about the identity crisis that has left many Muslims estranged from both a modernity imposed upon them and a tradition subverted for nationalist and Islamist purposes.

Mohammed Arkoun is professor emeritus of Islamic thought at the Sorbonne. **Robert D. Lee** is professor of political science at Colorado College.

3734 018

Praise for
RETHINKING ISLAM

"Arkoun's bold reassessment challenges both Western and Muslim scholarship in a comprehensive and at times provocative rethinking of Islamic history and thought. If there has been an Islamic resurgence, its thrust has been in terms of social and political activism. A concomitant challenge is the intellectual reformation or reformulation of the Islamic tradition. While some progress has been made, few have attempted as comprehensive and systematic a reexamination. The author has identified many of the most pressing themes and issues and rigorously addressed them. The book will generate 'light and heat' and attract a broad audience of readers concerned with contemporary Islam, Muslim thought, and intellectual history."

—*John L. Esposito*
Georgetown University

"*Rethinking Islam* is an inspiring and provocative book. Most Islamicists dismiss any rethinking of Islam as heresy. For Arkoun truth is always shaped by history, and Islam is no exception. Arkoun wants to be viewed neither as a modernist nor as a secularist, but as an intellectual who despises equally the anti-intellectualism of Islamic fundamentalists who subordinate reason to faith and the Eurocentrism of Western Orientalists. Arkoun puts things in his 'Arkounian way.' He does not say, for example, that Islam and human rights are in conflict but simply states, 'One ought not to expect of religions more than they can give.' It is high time that American readers are exposed to the thoughts of this unique Muslim intellectual."

—*Bassam Tibi*
University of Göttingen

"Arkoun is the leading thinker in the effort to articulate the Islamic message in global contemporary terms. He goes beyond old ethnocentric battles and provides the intellectual foundations for transcending the clash of civilizations. This is a very significant presentation of those ideas. For anyone who wants to go beyond the headlines and stereotypes about contemporary Islam, this book is absolutely essential reading."

—*John Voll*
University of New Hampshire

For order and other information, please write to:

WESTVIEW PRESS

5500 Central Avenue
Boulder, Colorado 80301-2877

36 Lonsdale Road
Summertown • Oxford OX2 7EW

ISBN 0-8133-2294-4

90000

9 780813 322940